COMPETITIVENESS
The Executive's
Guide to
SUCCE$$

COMPETITIVENESS
The Executive's
Guide to
SUCCESS

L. WILLIAM SEIDMAN
STEVEN L. SKANCKE

M. E. SHARPE, INC.
Armonk, New York
London, England

Copyright © 1989 by M. E. Sharpe, Inc.
80 Business Park Drive, Armonk, New York 10504.

Available in the United Kingdom and Europe from M. E. Sharpe,
Publishers, 3 Henrietta Street, London WC2E 8LU.

Interior design by Sonja Godfried

Library of Congress Cataloging-in-Publication Data

Seidman, Lewis William, 1921–
    Competitiveness—the executive's guide to success.

    1. Competition.   2. Industrial management.
I. Skancke, Steven L.   II. Title.
HD41.S39   1989   658.4   87-36172
ISBN 0-87332-475-7

Printed in the United States of America

CONTENTS

PREFACE
J. Peter Grace

Competitiveness: The Executive's Guide to Success will be of interest to all those who want to win by doing their job in a better way. Written for managers at all levels, it is aimed primarily at the private sector, but it certainly will be just as useful for those who work in federal, state, or local governments.

Increasing productivity is the only way American companies can meet the growing challenge from foreign competition. It is also the key to raising living standards in America. For a country, higher productivity means higher spendable income and the opportunity to use the increase in overall prosperity to expand public services without raising taxes. For a company, higher productivity means lower costs, better pricing advantages, greater competitiveness, and higher net income.

A wide variety of factors has contributed to the rise in foreign competition. Not least among them is high federal deficits that reduce the pool of private savings available for use in buying productivity improvements. Though individual companies and their managers can do little by themselves to reduce federal deficits or cure other national problems, they can do a great deal to improve their own competitive position by increasing the value of the goods and services they produce with the resources they have at hand.

As this book points out, managers play a vital role in combining productive people with productive investment to make a better product. How well they manage to do this will determine how well their companies fare and, ultimately, whether they will be able to maintain jobs for themselves and their fellow employees.

In this book, the authors provide an interesting blend of new and time-honored techniques for increasing productivity. More importantly, however, they describe ideas and initiatives that are now being used successfully in companies across America. In fact, many case studies of how productivity-increasing ideas have been implemented successfully provide the backbone of the book. Whether you are interested in knowing how to create a better reward system or how to ignite a computer revolution, you will find good examples to emulate here.

I have been a chief executive officer in the private sector for many years, during which time I have tried to keep up on ideas for improving performance. But I was surprised at the number of new and practical ideas for improving productivity that I found in this book. Equally important is how Seidman and Skancke use these examples to remind us that improved productivity and thus competitiveness depends very much on businesspeople treating others as they would like to be treated—the Golden Rule. Managers need to recognize the benefits of developing partnerships and a sense of shared destiny among employees, suppliers, and even customers.

I found this book a refreshing departure from the recent surge of management books that focus only on one manager's experience or on a limited number of companies that have been extraordinarily successful. *Competitiveness: The Executive's Guide to Success* synthesizes and highlights what a highly diverse group of companies is doing to improve their own productivity, competitiveness, and profitability.

The authors have included in the Appendix excerpts from the Report of the White House Conference on Productivity for those readers who are interested in knowing more about what business, labor, academic, and government experts think ought to be done to raise productivity in America.

ACKNOWLEDGMENTS

We gratefully acknowledge the extraordinary efforts of those who have contributed to the quality and timeliness of the information provided in *Competitiveness: The Executive's Guide to Success*. Many managers provided direction for this project by telling us what they needed most in a handbook. Many readers from the workplace provided helpful and encouraging comments, and many successful companies were willing to share the formulas they found for improving their competitiveness.

A very special thanks is also due those who worked with us in assembling and verifying information about companies, and in editing and typing the manuscript: Patricia Pate, Kevin Prins, James Reinsel, Marilyn Rudick, and Nancy Skancke. Doyle Pickett, Sally Seidman, and Nancy Skancke were invaluable in helping us see this project through to publication.

*A competitor is the guy who goes in a revolving
door behind you and comes out ahead of you.*
—*George Romney*
*Former Governor of Michigan
and CEO of American Motors*

INTRODUCTION

Survival of the fittest is the dominant theme today in the jungle of unregulated world competition. In this new, no-holds-barred battleground, in which the soldiers are businesses, governments, cartels, and ideologies, America's corporate managers must be tougher, leaner, and more skilled. To succeed, in short, they must become the best competitors.

Our search for America's best ideas for improving competitiveness has led us through the academic, government, and corporate sectors. Although service in government does not usually provide many opportunities for viewing the best side of private enterprise, we were lucky enough to observe some companies at their competitive best when we directed the White House Conference on Productivity. As a result, we had the unique opportunity to study a wide range of American companies and their creative ideas for improving profits and productivity.

Our observations and experiences are encouraging. We saw that many U.S. companies have become real competitors in the global marketplace, and that they are teeming with successful, proven ideas for raising profits and improving their competitive edge through productivity.

The ideas we are writing about have brought a multitude of changes in the way Americans do business. By incorporating and adapting some of these productive strategies, you may find an exciting and dynamic revolution in your own workplace.

Through the White House Conference on Productivity, we were able to conduct a broad investigation of American business to uncover the profit-making innovations already under way in established companies. In addition, hundreds of other firms volunteered to share their ideas through computer teleconferencing, workshops, and the development of case studies. America's top competitors were proud to bring their successful formulas to our attention, and we have used the time since the conference to evaluate how these ideas have endured.

Successful innovations abound in every part of American business—in every kind of enterprise and in every facet of operations. Over and over again, we hear successful managers giving the same advice:

> Quality means productivity.
> Automate! Emigrate! or Evaporate!
> Communicate!
> Organize listening.
> Sine emptor, nullum negotium! (No customer, no business.)
> Bring high tech to the low tech and old tech.
> The Golden Rule is still golden.
> Productivity is management.

Some managers recite these phrases without reflecting on them, while others have made them a part of their business culture. Implementing these ideas requires thoughtful action. Becoming more profitable and more competitive means managing all resources better—including your own time—and teamwork improves the effort. Successful competitors work with all employees, including organized labor. Suppliers become partners with producers, and would-be contenders are seeing the benefit of cooperating where necessary to beat world-class foreign competition.

Recognizing the value of employees is also a critical element in today's changing marketplace. Successful companies everywhere have recognized that their employees are the key to their growth and success. Training and development, as well as research, innovation, and technology, are key ingredients for survival; they are necessary and productive investments.

Companies in the vanguard of world-class competition, those with good profits and rising productivity, are not there by accident. They have leaders who plan and organize for their success, who know where the company is heading, and who communicate their strategy all the way down the line. They make sure that their organization is flexible and that decisions can be made quickly in the midst of battle. After all, that is what counts when you are locked in the heat of competition.

The old saying "There is nothing new under the sun" applies to some of the ideas we have been gathering. But rediscovery can sometimes be just as useful as finding out about ideas for the first time. And some of these strategies belie the old saying by being truly innovative.

Among the companies that have used the old and the new to gain the competitive advantage are:

Diamond Fiber Products. Implementing a comprehensive program for rewarding employees who do their job well, Diamond increased output 16.5 percent and accrued savings of $5 million in only eighteen months.

Como Plastics Corporation. By adopting a people-oriented approach to management that emphasizes teamwork, Como doubled sales and increased profits over 800 percent during a three-year period.

Donnelly Corporation. Applying a variety of reward systems over a seven-year period, including profit sharing and participative management, Donnelly reaped a 220-percent return on investment.

Certified Grocers. By adopting suggestions made by its employees—and by rewarding outstanding workers with paid time off—Certified increased its productivity by 15 percent in one year, while saving more than $2 million in payroll costs.

Champion International. Organized into problem-solving teams, Champion's employees solved stubborn productivity-related issues that saved the company $7 million in the paper division alone.

Lowe's Companies, Inc. By making employees owners through ESOPs, Lowe's transformed itself into one of America's fastest growing corporations. Within three decades, it grew from three stores to more than 200, while boosting profits from $18 million to $900 million.

Palatine (Illinois) Police Department. Providing an alternative to traditional promotions through a dual-career ladder, the Palatine Police Department found a new way to motivate police personnel and increased productivity by 10 percent.

In spite of a steady stream of examples like these, however, some people still find the search for better productivity boring. Perhaps they should not, because it may be their salvation. Productivity is the cornerstone of our American entrepreneurial system and the foundation for our competitive position in the world. Our productivity as a nation determines how well we live, for rising productivity remains the only "free lunch" in economics.

Though the U.S. still has one of the highest levels of productivity in the world, its rate of improvement in recent years has fallen well below the leading industrialized countries.

In fact, foreign competition has emerged today as the dominant issue facing U.S. business. The survival of many major industries and an increasing number of smaller ones depends on improving productivity so that we can compete with foreign producers. This reality has become all too clear to the steel, auto, chemical, paper, mining, sugar, agriculture, and textile industries.

Our look at U.S. competitiveness has convinced us that American companies still have what it takes to meet world-class competition head on and to be number one. The opportunity to raise productivity, to become a first-class competitor, and to earn higher profits is still available for anyone willing to take up the challenge.

HOW TO USE THIS BOOK

This book is organized into ten chapters to make it easy to peruse those areas you think might offer you the greatest chance for improving your own competitive position. We have tried to demonstrate many of our ideas with examples from business and government. Should you want to delve more deeply into any of these ideas, short case studies are included at the back of the book, as well as the name, address, and telephone number of a company contact. Not every company mentioned in this book is an example of overall excellence, but all of them have been successful in developing and using some idea to improve productivity, profits, and competitive position in today's business world.

Throughout this book we have included statements made by competitors we have worked with in our search for new ideas. They reflect the way successful competitors think and act and we believe they will give you a better understanding of what the pros are doing.

COMPETITIVENESS
The Executive's
Guide to
SUCCE$$

*Productivity is everybody's business, but most
particularly, a manager's.*
—John Grant, Manager
TRW Space and Technology Group

1

MANAGERS:
Thirteen Guidelines for Competing

To be a successful competitor, you have to be a successful manager, and a
successful manager is a leader. But what is a leader? Though definitions and
descriptions vary, almost all managers agree that a leader is someone who sets an
example for others to follow. Rather than trying to identify leadership traits
through "empirical" studies, we listened to successful managers talk about their
own guidelines for leadership. From the hundreds of testimonies we gathered,
certain themes emerged.

1. KNOW WHERE YOU ARE GOING AND HOW YOU PLAN TO GET THERE. BE FLEXIBLE AND PERSISTENT IN THE PURSUIT OF DEFINED GOALS.

Let workers know what your objectives are—both short-term and long-term. The
old adage "If you don't know where you're going, any road will do" is true on
the factory floor, as well as the boardroom. Nothing is more important than
mobilizing everyone toward a common goal.

2. FIRST THINGS FIRST EVERY DAY.

Decide each day what is most important in terms of meeting your objectives. Get
organized and disciplined. Make a "To Do" list at the start of each day, then do
the hardest, least pleasant tasks first.

3. MEASURE EVERYONE'S PRODUCTIVITY, INCLUDING YOUR OWN!

Unless you are measuring your productivity, you will not know whether you are on course, off course, or ready to crash. Measures can and should be simple. The best are usually the ones developed by the individuals or groups being measured. In fact, many managers and employees already have informal measures that they subconsciously use to answer questions like "Why do I deserve a raise or a promotion?" or "Why should I promote this employee instead of another?"

But try not to get bogged down in the trappings of an intricate measurement system. No system is worth extraordinary hours or costs, so use data that already exist or can be easily assembled.

4. BE A MOBILE COMMUNICATOR.

Walk around, talk, look, listen, and spread the word. When you are confined to your office, you do not have access to your most valuable asset: your people. Communication also means listening, so let your employees know that you want to hear from them, and then hear them out.

The key to communication is attitude. A "Be reasonable, do it my way" approach will not make the grade. Be willing to become a partner in a joint process, not a commander in the field. Partnership is not an abdication of authority, but rather a productivity tool. Time after time, managers usually find that it is the front-line worker who knows more about how to correct productivity problems than anyone else.

One very difficult thing for a manager to do is to drop the natural defense mechanism. Instead of letting your mind automatically generate "why we do it this way," a manager should try to see the issue from the side of the person asking the question. Being mobile also means being able to move 180 degrees to the other side of the situation.

5. COORDINATE AND CONTROL.

Managers must coordinate procedures, processes, and people. They must be able to provide integration, leadership, and delegate responsibility. The manager's ability to coordinate and control the operation is, in the end, the reason that the product turns out to be the desired horse instead of the proverbial camel.

Control does not necessarily mean centralized decision making, but it does mean a certain amount of supervision. And a manager's methods of supervision must constantly be revised, because each day brings new challenges as people and production methods change.

6. COMPUTERS ARE THE KEY TO PRODUCTIVITY IMPROVEMENT.

Computers are the most important new tool for enhancing productivity. Whether you are involved in manufacturing or a service industry or are self-employed, computers can provide information, control operations, and monitor quality at a relatively low cost.

Being technologically aware and up-to-date is a major challenge. As computers are made more inexpensive, more powerful, and more "user friendly," they will become an even more important component of future productivity plans.

7. SEEK OUT AND REMOVE OBSTACLES TO PRODUCTIVITY.

Let employees know that you are serious about eliminating productivity barriers by organizing a "search and destroy" mission. Ask all your people to list what they see as obstacles to *their own* productivity, then have them list the obstacles they see to the company's overall productivity and efficiency. When the problems are clearly identified, have the courage to remove them no matter whose territory is invaded.

8. REWARD YOUR PRODUCERS.

Employees are your greatest resource. Why not let them know it? Reward those who help you, and not just by fattening their paychecks. Peer recognition, for example, is a powerful motivator, so capitalize on it.

And remember, gainsharing has no net cost. Employee ownership contributes to a sense of common fate, because all owners have a vested interest in making their organization work.

9. ENCOURAGE INNOVATION, EVEN IF YOU HAVE TO RUFFLE A FEW FEATHERS.

Entrepreneurs are created by working with entrepreneurs, because the acceptance of new ideas forces learning and change. The biggest paybacks come from ideas that change the product, the process, and the people.

Productivity gains require innovation, change, flexibility, and adaptability. Every good system borrows from the past and attempts to innovate for the future, and each problem requires its own solution. "We always did it that way" is a sure formula for frozen productivity and the loss of competitive position.

10. EXPECT AND ACCEPT ONLY QUALITY.

To achieve quality, you must ask for it, expect it, require it, and reward it. Excellence breeds excellence. Without quality, you will not have any customers, and without customers, you will not have a business.

11. BE ENTHUSIASTIC.

A happy environment is a productive environment, so play the company cheerleader and emphasize a can-do approach to work. Remember enthusiasm is contagious, but so is defeatism. So learn to accept problems as opportunities, not as harbingers of doom and despair.

12. ACT NOW!

Fix it, move it, try it, explore it, and go for it. We seldom fail for lack of good ideas, but we will always fail if we do not act on them. So be opportunistic and take risks. Set deadlines, and if you miss them, set new ones. Above all, act!

13. STAY HEALTHY; BE HAPPY.

Energetic management requires a healthy body and a sound mind. No job is worth endangering your health, so stay in good physical shape and leave your worries at the company doorstep. And encourage your employees to stay healthy too.

Feel free to integrate these guidelines into your management style one by one and embellish them with your own imagination and specialized knowledge. As in golf—where you have to keep your left arm straight, head down, eye on the ball, shift your weight, and follow through—learning them all may seem like a lot to handle in one lesson.

It's not what top management says, it's what it does that counts.
—Bob Cowie, Senior Vice President
Dana Corporation

2

ORGANIZATION:
Getting Ready for the Competition

Becoming a winner does not happen by accident. If you want to win—to be productive, profitable, and competitive—then you have to organize yourself to make it happen. Although techniques for getting organized may vary widely, we have identified ten organizational maxims common to companies that have successfully become productive competitors.

1. PRODUCTIVITY PROGRAMS START AT THE TOP.

Without the endorsement of senior management, no productivity plan can really succeed, no competition can be won. "You have to say it at the top and mean it all the way down," says Don Gross of Certified Grocers of California, a grocery wholesaler. The Dana Corporation, a vehicular components manufacturer with thousands of employees, demonstrates its concern for productivity by making sure that every employee meets with a senior-level manager at least once a year. And the company chairman lets everyone know of his concerns, goals, and personal views through a quarterly letter to employees. At Prince Corporation, an auto parts manufacturer, President John Spoelhof shows his support and concern by personally reviewing 70 to 80 percent of all quarterly personnel reports.

2. MORE PRODUCTIVITY MEANS FEWER LAYERS.

Reducing management layers not only lowers overall costs, it also enhances communication. You've heard the saying: "With each layer of management, 50 percent of the message being passed down the line is lost." Today, the spokes of the wheel are replacing the pyramid as the structure most widely copied by productive organizations. It allows for stronger participation, increased input, and greater consideration of a wide variety of viewpoints.

"One steel company has thirty-two levels of management between the first-line supervisor and the senior executive," says Carla O'Dell, a Houston-based management consultant. Compare that to Apple Computer: "We [had] three levels of management—and I was one of them," said Steven Jobs, the company's founder who currently is leading a new entrepreneurial enterprise.

3. A WELL-DEVISED PRODUCTIVITY PLAN SPREADS ACCOUNTABILITY THROUGHOUT THE ORGANIZATION.

Pushing responsibility down the organizational ladder to the "hands-on" working level is a common ingredient of many successful productivity plans. "Never tell people how to do things, tell them what to do and they will surprise you with their ingenuity," says one savvy manager. "Delegation goes all the way down the line to the key person—the most important manager of all—that is, the person who actually produces the product."

At American Seating, one of the largest producers of seating, responsibility for setting production goals rests with cost-reduction committees. These committees set their own goals for productivity improvement and determine a monetary value for the savings they hope to achieve. Once these goals are defined, the committee sets out to accomplish them as it sees fit, purchasing new machines, or redesigning production lines, if necessary.

At Comsonics, a Virginia cable TV products firm, all employees are stockholders; they are, therefore, considered one of the four levels of management and are expected to help in making important management decisions. For example, when the diagnostic and repair areas faced the problem of too little space, too little time, and too much work, a worker committee came up with a solution—adding a third shift with a 12 percent pay differential—even though it meant that some other workers would lose their overtime pay.

4. COMPETITIVENESS IS AN INTEGRAL PART OF THE CORPORATE CULTURE.

Improving your competitiveness requires more than a new organizational chart, it requires a change in attitude. And this attitude must be reflected in your corporate culture. After all, corporate culture is what defines acceptable behavior, and a culture that integrates change, innovation, risk taking, cooperation, and quality is one that will lead to productivity improvement.

Competitive managers are those who work to define and create the type of corporate culture that breeds productivity. "Create an organization where people share a sense of common fate—that is, a common productivity ethic," says one manager. "A corporate culture that develops a sharp pain in anyone who sees waste or inefficiency is the kind of attitude you want," explains another.

At Dana, the corporate culture constantly reflects the company's strong confidence in the individual. "We have a lot of folk sayings around here," notes a top official, "and one of them is that within your own twenty-five square feet, the person doing the job is the one who knows the most about it, and he's the expert. It's an attitude that's not easy to develop, but once you've got it, it's a marvelous tool."

Westinghouse decided to adopt a corporate culture that emphasized cooperation. Time and motion study experts—traditionally hated figures in U.S. factories—began working with, not *on*, employees, and the results were immediate and obvious. "We began to see an unquantifiable but undeniably real improvement in the quality of work life around the division. Many people have indicated that they're more satisfied now with the scope and challenge of their job. We haven't undertaken a formal attitude survey, but the feedback is extremely positive. In the elevators and on the stairways, we hear remarks like, 'I'm getting a lot more work done,' and 'My job's more interesting now.'"

Another good attitude to encourage concerns labor unions: rather than working against them, adopt a corporate culture that fosters cooperation. At the Joint Labor Management Committee (JLMC) of the Retail Foods Industry, for instance, the corporate culture promotes a new awareness and sensitivity to labor problems. As a result, there is a less hostile atmosphere in collective bargaining.

5. SUCCESSFUL PRODUCTIVITY PROGRAMS EVOLVE PIECE BY PIECE.

Organizing for productivity requires action at all levels and in all parts of the business, but it cannot be done all at once. In fact, crash programs of productivity are not likely to succeed. Start small and build from there. Test your idea with a small group before you implement it companywide. Each of the ideas in this book is a good place to start: people, technology, attitudes, or strategies. Successful programs are built by pieces and evolve as required.

Diamond Fiber Products provides a good example of how to introduce change slowly. When Diamond conceived of the idea of the "100 Club" as a means of rewarding outstanding employees through recognition and gifts, it cautiously introduced the program at its egg carton plant in Palmer, Massachusetts. The company's investment in both time and money was modest, but when an evaluation revealed impressive results—both in productivity (output increased 16.5 percent) and attitude (grievances declined 43 percent)—Diamond introduced the club into four of its other plants. Success in these additional plants proved that this was an innovation worthy of expansion. As of today, Personnel Manager Dan

Boyle has installed sixty similar programs in manufacturing and service organizations around the country.

6. PRODUCTIVITY PROGRAMS ARE CUSTOMER- AND QUALITY-ORIENTED.

Customers are the reason for any business, and today they demand quality and service. Keeping the customer satisfied is the price you have to pay for your continued existence.

Good quality requires the effective management of systems and processes. As one financial officer explains: "It's interesting to note that purely human mistakes are only a small minority of the errors that reduce quality in our business. In fact, less than 15 percent of the source of error derives from our account officers or operators, while 85 percent of the problems stem from the system—technological foul-ups or lack of communication. In other words, 85 percent of the errors require management action for prevention. Workers are really powerless in solving the bulk of the problems."

Productivity and quality are really two sides of the same coin. Productivity improves when there is an organized effort to equate quality with productivity, and poor quality can destroy any productivity program.

7. CONSIDERATION BREEDS SUCCESS.

Respectful, considerate, and even gentlemanly conduct between managers and workers is a common characteristic found in successful organizations. For Warren Braun, chief executive officer at Comsonics, consideration means treating everyone "as I would like to be treated." At Kollmorgen, a manufacturer of printed circuits, Chairman Bob Swiggett notes: "We just assume that everybody's honest, and we run the business that way." Explains one company official, "We preach trust and the Golden Rule, and we're very careful that what we do is the same as what we say. Once we had a book that said you get three days off if your mother or father dies, but if a neighbor dies that you've known for thirty-five years, you get no time off. We threw the book out."

Productivity gains are dependent upon the motivation of people, and their enthusiasm and commitment to corporate goals depends upon the way they are treated. Consideration for others is the only way to create a winning team.

8. THERE IS ALWAYS A BETTER WAY TO ACHIEVE THE SAME RESULTS.

"The way we always do it" may not be the best way to do it now. With new technologies and new methods of management being developed every day, the old way may very well be obsolete. It is important to examine every detail of your operation to determine if there is a better, more efficient way of doing things. Often there are better ways to managing the talents of others, reorganize, or simply change the way jobs are done.

Kollmorgen found that breaking units down into smaller sizes, for instance, helped transform its photocircuits operation. Prior to its merger with Kollmorgen, Photocircuits Corporation had been a pioneer in the manufacture of printed circuit boards. But one day, when Kollmorgen's chairman, Bob Swiggett, surveyed the production floor—500 workers, fifty process steps, fifteen departments, and 100 open orders—he realized that the operations were in fact "a classic case of confusion . . .[they] were lucky ever to ship anything."

In an attempt to solve this problem, Kollmorgen installed an elegant and expensive computerized control and production system. The computer worked beautifully, but the company's performance got worse. Foremen were preoccupied with printouts instead of people, and managers spent more time worrying about the internal systems than about customers.

Recognizing that the computer system had not eliminated the confusion, only computerized it, Swiggett went to the concept of small teams that had seemed to work so well in the old expediting department. Dividing the entire company into groups of about seventy-five people organized along product line or market segment, Swiggett made each team responsible for its own small profit center. "Almost magically," explains Swiggett, "everything improved. Customers were happier, pricing was better, profits rose, inventories turned faster, troublesome book-to-physical-inventory variance surprises disappeared. Morale rose with the evidence of success." After six months of the new decentralized system, output per employee had doubled and on-time deliveries improved from 60 to 90 percent.

Work simplification is another, often overlooked approach for improving substantial benefits. When Como Plastics took a careful look at its assembly line, for example, it found that it could redesign the line to use one less employee and still achieve the same output. At Great Salt Lake Mineral and Chemical Corporation, a minor change of rotating shifts forward instead of backward—in tune with worker's circadian rhythms—helped to keep shift employees awake and more productive.

Work simplification often requires no more than eliminating bureaucratic regulations that developed and multiplied over the years and that may no longer be relevant. "Thirteen years ago," explains an official at Dana, "we had three volumes that defined our standard operating procedures. We threw them out. And there's an interesting story that goes along with that. It was our then president who decided that he'd really like to try a different way of running the company, so he went into the chairman with this armload of books and he said, 'Say, I want to throw these out.' And the chairman said, 'Oh no, you can't do that, that's good stuff. You know it cost us a lot of money to develop it.' So the president said, 'Well, all right, you tell me what the good stuff is and I'll keep that.' The chairman replied, 'Well, I don't know, I've never read the darn thing.' "

9. JUDICIOUS INVESTMENTS MUST BE MADE IN EQUIPMENT, COMPUTERS, NEW TECHNIQUES, AND TECHNOLOGIES.

In today's increasingly competitive business world, it is essential to evaluate and plan for sound capital investments. Again and again, successful companies have found that wise investments in technology pay for themselves many times over.

At Reynolds Aluminum, a $125 million overhaul in the cold running mill at its McCook aluminum steel and plate plant in Brookfield, Illinois increased employee output by 100 percent. The use of robots in GE's Daytona plant increased productivity by reducing errors and defects 42 percent.

For the Calvert Group, which manages financial funds, investing in better telecommunications—long-distance 800 numbers, watts lines, and a sophisticated phone system that monitors the length of calls, and the number of calls "on hold"—allowed the company to manage its customers more efficiently. Now, employees know when to speed up their phone interactions because they always know just how many customers are waiting to be served.

10. GOOD TRAINING ASSURES THE SUCCESS OF PRODUCTIVITY PROGRAMS.

Training on a continuing basis is the hallmark of a good competitor with a sound productivity program. The auto industry, for example, has become a leader in implementing innovative training programs. At General Motor's Orion, Michigan, plant, workers and supervisors participated in an intensive three-week training course on teamwork and quality control that was designed to facilitate employee acceptance of a plant-wide technological upgrade. With an emphasis on changing attitudes toward technology and on teaching new skills, workers were trained in multi-task assembly operations. When the training was completed, a fully qualified worker could perform all the jobs in one part of the assembly line, enabling that person to fill in for other workers when the need arose.

A competitor, Ford Motor Company, is equally committed to training. It has teamed up with the United Auto Workers to form the Ford Employee Development and Training Program. The fifteen plus courses it provides are designed to increase employee skills, productivity, and quality of life, and retrain furloughed employees for new jobs.

Training is essential for managers as well as labor. Champion International, a large conglomerate, identifies managers with high potential and places them in its "Managing for Excellence" program. At Hughes Aircraft, managers are trained not only to develop an understanding of productivity, but also to foster a dedicated commitment to productivity improvement.

If you don't know where you're going, any road will get you there.

—Alice in Wonderland

3

PLANNING:
Strategies for Staying Ahead

Harland Cleveland* has defined strategic planning as the act of "innovating around a general sense of direction." The words "general sense of direction" are a key component of this definition, because no one has yet devised a way to plan in detail very far into the future. The future, perhaps fortunately, will always remain a mystery.

The primary objective in setting a direction is to move ahead of the crowd or, as it is usually called, "getting ahead of the curve." This concept is at the heart of the planning process and is the foundation for short-term, detailed planning that is necessary for improving productivity and competitive position.

It is top management's responsibility to ascertain what road to take—to define the "general direction." In order to do that, management needs to listen to employees and customers to make sure it is not heading down a dead-end street. Once the general direction is determined, managers must then work to develop flexible strategies that can anticipate and respond to the inevitable changes in the marketplace.

If defining a general sense of direction is all there is to strategic planning, then why is so much attention paid to it? Because defining where to take the organization is the most important decision management must make.

Often companies within the same industry will make vastly different strategic

---

*Formerly President of the University of Hawaii; currently Director of the Hubert H. Humphrey Institute at the University of Minnesota, St. Paul, Minnesota.

planning decisions. In the steel industry, for example, many companies have had to choose whether to remain solely in the steel business or to diversify. Bethlehem Steel has decided to devote itself almost exclusively to the manufacturing and processing of steel, while U.S. Steel, by contrast, has decided to expand in other directions. Having set their basic course, however, both companies now must make future decisions based on this initial choice. The "general direction" is the signpost that affects each and every turn.

Once a company has defined its strategic plan, it can then explore proposals and actions designed to move the enterprise in that direction. No numbers are needed in this exercise, only ideas. The company must attempt to determine where its customers, its industry, and the general economy are headed, then move to take advantage of the changing environment.

KNOW THY CUSTOMER

How is this seemingly overwhelming feat achieved? Primarily through the knowledge and satisfaction of customer needs. That is why you have to study your customer thoroughly and ask yourself: What can be done to make my customer a happier person? Only by anticipating trends and directions, or even by creating new trends, can you get the jump on the competition. Frederick Webster, Jr., at Dartmouth's Tuck School of Business, puts it this way: "The most basic commitment of all must be to the customer: commitment to quality products and services, and innovative timely solutions to customer problems." Knowing how to satisfy the customer can be the result of field work, marketing studies, personal observation, good guesswork, or even intuition. But no matter where it comes from, your knowledge of your customer is the key to improving your competitive position through planning.

BECOME MORE FLEXIBLE

No plan to satisfy the customer will work forever. Your customers operate in a dynamic environment, and their needs and desires change quickly. And since no one can accurately forecast the future, all strategic plans will involve some degree of risk.

An essential ingredient of good planning, therefore, is flexibility. Nothing is more destructive to a company's success than turning the strategy of today into an inviolate rule for tomorrow. The ultimate test of the quality of your planning is your ability to perceive that the weather has changed and you need to set a new course.

And often strategies must be altered quickly in spite of substantial resistance. Decisions to veer toward one direction rather than another, or even to make a U-turn, may cause conflicts among sales, product development, and manufacturing. For instance, it is not uncommon to hear the production chiefs complaining: "We just got this line running right, and now the guys in sales want to change it—and in forty-eight hours.''

The need for quick change often results from a surprise market development or the introduction of a new product by a competitor. But even though changing quickly can be expensive, not changing quickly enough can be even more expensive. As an ancient Chinese proverb says, ''If we can't change directions, we shall end up where we are headed.''

Flexibility, then, becomes the watchword of those who must design, manufacture, or distribute the product, and a system of ''planning for change'' is essential. Technology can make ''instant'' change possible, because flexible manufacturing systems can reduce set-up times for production lines from weeks to minutes. But managers themselves have to embrace the concept of flexibility first before new technology can provide any advantage in the marketplace.

TUNE IN TO CHANGE

Many companies credit their success to the ability to combine an understanding of the customer's changing needs with organizational flexibility. Federal Express, for instance, sized up the information explosion and perceived a real need to move information faster from place to place. The result was overnight package delivery—the first in the country. Other companies now provide the same service, but by getting there first, Federal Express set the pace in the competition and has continued to run well ahead of the pack.

Both Carl Eller, chairman of Circle K convenience stores, and Robert Anderson, chairman of ARCO, examined customer needs and perceived a new trend in convenience shopping. They saw that consumers wanted two commodities—gasoline and groceries—at one location. So Circle K redesigned its convenience stores to include gas pumps, while ARCO added convenience stores to its filling stations.

The communications industry also produced its share of visionaries who beat the competition by anticipating customer needs. Since the beginning of radio, for example, many people had been losing money or going broke attempting to put new FM stations on the air. Even though FM broadcasting offered clear stereo reception, AM radio had become the industry standard. In fact, most of the public did not have FM receivers.

This situation, however, changed in the mid–1960s. Visionary broadcasters noticed a change under way when Japanese manufacturers began selling AM-FM radio receivers as a strategy to penetrate the U.S. market. At the time, there were no ''takers'' for over 400 FM licenses available from the Federal Communications Commission (FCC), even in fast growing markets of the country—Aspen, Colorado, and Orlando, Florida. But then the ''beat-the-crowd'' strategists made their move into FM radio, and the same FM licenses that went begging in 1970 are worth hundreds of millions of dollars today.

Television provides another vivid example. In the fifties and sixties, the major networks dominated the television market, attracting both mass audiences and advertiser dollars, while independent and UHF stations were, for the most part, unprofitable. Broadcasters saw little reason to invest in these alternatives, which were generally perceived to be losers. Because of low demand, these licenses could be acquired from the FCC inexpensively and without costly and time-consuming competitive applications.

By 1976, the situation in the TV industry had changed. By providing an array of new channels, cable television had changed viewing patterns and many TV watchers were beginning to prefer counterprogramming. With network domination broken, independent stations that offered something different suddenly attracted sizeable audiences and became very profitable. In Phoenix, Arizona, for example, anyone "ahead of the crowd" could obtain the license for Channel 15 for practically nothing. But ten years later, this "free" license had a value of more than $30 million.

This scenario was repeated across the country. In 1976, UHF licenses in small markets like Albany, San Antonio, and Omaha were awarded without competition. But by 1978, the few licenses that were still available in these cities were heavily contested—with between eight and ten bidders competing for each application. Being just a year or two ahead of the curve made the profitable difference.

FIND YOUR NICHE

In the end, your company's resources are best spent when you know best where to spend them. Profits are greatest when you alone have the right product, are producing it with the best combination of people, capital, and materials, and know how to sell it to anyone for whom it has real value. Successful planning focuses on finding your niche and making it profitable, while higher productivity is one of the objectives of planning. The ultimate goal is a successfully competitive and profitable enterprise.

Quality is job one!
—John Manoogian, General Manager
Ford Motor Company

4

QUALITY:
An Overlooked Strategy for Success

Few successful managers know any Latin, but most of them have heard the saying *sine emptor nullum negotium*—"without a customer, you have no business." If you want to compete, you have to please your customers. And nothing pleases customers more than dealing with a vendor who sells a *quality* product at a reasonable price.

In many American companies, however, the emphasis has been placed on volume at the expense of quality. And as a result, the goods and services offered by these companies have developed a reputation for mediocrity even though many of them were once considered the best in the world. This has occurred in large part because quality standards have slipped from "high" to merely "acceptable," because many companies don't understand that quality is essentially free. IBM rigorously promotes the concept of quality being free, as do other companies. Even though a company may spend more on statistical quality control procedures, the net result is lower costs and overall savings. IBM, Hewlett-Packard, Ford, and others mentioned here involve their suppliers as well in quality control and thus multiply the beneficial impact on competitiveness.

TAKING IT FROM THE TOP

The commitment to quality requires high standards of performance in everything a company does. From the chief executive officer to those who sweep the floors, only the best performance should be considered good enough. Bruce Hill, a vice president of Olin Corporation, a brass fabricating company, explains his approach to quality this way: "Quality is everything that goes with having a satisfied and, hopefully, a continuing customer. It's not just product quality; it's the quality of service, of responsiveness, and of error-free delivery."

If suppliers provide quality materials and workers prepare quality products, then sales forces can market more with less effort. If quality is a top priority, then every step of the production process requires less effort and results in more goods at lower cost. Sales and profits come naturally when quality and productivity work together.

Step one in improving quality is the commitment of senior management. "Unless you receive the support of the CEO and president," one executive told us, "you're not going to get to first base. Your commitment to quality should be reflected throughout your company, from the purchasing specifications given to parts and material suppliers all the way through to the delivery of the final product."

Olin Corporation has had first-hand experience with how a commitment to quality at the top pays off in productivity. When the company discovered that its customers viewed Olin products as merely "satisfactory," it decided to make quality a top priority. Senior-level managers went down the line to every worker and explained how things were going to change. They emphasized that inferior quality was no longer acceptable, and that Olin could not survive without making a commitment to producing only the best.

Once the message was heard and accepted, things began to happen quickly. Special task forces were assembled to find new ways to improve product quality, while workers at all levels became involved in identifying and correcting situations that contributed to lower quality production. The company trained employees to manage quality assurance programs and practice statistical quality control.

As a result of this commitment, the quality of Olin's products began to improve significantly. Customers clearly were more satisfied, and within five years, product rejections dropped by 83 percent. In one product line that accounted for $14 million in sales, Olin received only $154 worth of returned merchandise. At the same time, the quality of work life improved for all Olin employees, and union grievances against the company dropped dramatically.

DEFECT PREVENTION

For many companies, quality assurance means merely offering customers fix-it-after-the-sale warranties. Though these warranties may be better than nothing, they usually indicate that customers will have to endure product failure and become involved in the frustrating ordeal of getting a product repaired. When that happens, customers respond in a highly predictable way: they transfer their allegiance to a manufacturer who produces a better quality product.

The goal of "doing it right the first time" should belong to everyone. Company standards and incentives must reflect the commitment to quality, and the measure of an employee's worth must take into account the quality of performance. If an employee is not producing quality work, his or her evaluation and compensation should reflect that failure.

Everyone needs to be involved in the process of improving quality, even suppliers. When goods are received that do not meet company standards, suppliers should be penalized, while those who deliver quality goods should be rewarded with long-term contracts and preferential bidding. Working with quality-conscious suppliers saves you money in more ways than one. It not only eliminates all the delays and repairs resulting from having to work with inferior components, but it also eliminates the time you usually have to spend inspecting subcontractor parts.

The Ford Motor Company provides a dramatic example of how the commitment to doing things right the first time can enhance productivity. Like most American auto manufacturers, Ford used to depend on a "reactive" quality control system that focused on finding and fixing problems as quickly as possible, rather than on preventing them. All too often, however, the company did not react quickly enough and the customer ended up "owning" the problem. Eventually, these defects and breakdowns become unacceptable to consumers, especially with the advent of high-quality foreign imports.

To remedy the situation, Ford hired a new quality assurance director and charged him with the task of putting quality back into Ford cars. He launched an all-out effort, organizing workers into reliability teams and training them to understand quality control and how to build a better car. Design and assembly engineers began to work together to use statistical control techniques to measure production variances, while Ford invested heavily in more advanced technology, introducing computer-controlled flexible manufacturing systems to reduce product variability. The company even included suppliers in its commitment to quality, and began recognizing those who delivered high-quality parts.

As a result of this companywide program, Ford made impressive gains in quality. In fact, a nationwide survey showed that the number of needed repairs dropped 59 percent for Ford cars and 47 percent for Ford trucks compared to three years earlier.

GETTING EMPLOYEES INVOLVED WITH QUALITY

Many workers will tell you that they would *like* to stress higher quality but that their managers seem to be a lot more concerned with throughput. Improving quality and increasing volume can sometimes appear to be conflicting goals, but if management expresses its commitment to both, perfection is possible.

One way to achieve it is to explain and demonstrate statistical sampling techniques and other methods of testing so employees can monitor their work in progress. Training them to do the job right with no margin for error will help to develop a cultural appreciation for why and how higher quality works for the good of all.

All employees should be involved in the quality program. That means asking them about the quality of the goods and services they produce and how they think the company can do a better job, and then acting on their suggestions. Another way to solicit employee support is through quality circles.

Quality circles can operate in many different ways. Employees who join can be assigned specific tasks relating to quality improvement, or the circle may operate with an open agenda, taking action and removing obstacles to quality and productivity wherever it finds them. We have already described how Olin convened quality circles to find solutions to their quality-related problems. Champion International and Donnelly Mirrors are companies that have also used these groups to boost their productivity substantially. Their successes are discussed in Chapter 7.

OTHER QUALITY STRATEGIES

There are many other strategies for improving quality, however, some of which are quite simple. Hertz, for example, instituted a policy of soliciting customer feedback on quality through customer questionnaires. And in the process of following up on these suggestions, the company reduced customer complaints to the lowest level in nine years.

Boeing Corporation relies on automation to improve the quality of its product. By computerizing the design, assembly, and inventory control of its aircraft manufacturing operations, the company has made it possible for engineers and assemblers to work together earlier to resolve design-related problems. Computerization also facilitates the assembly process by ensuring that the right components are on hand at the right time and in the right quantities. As a result of computerization, Boeing has not only improved quality, it has also reduced costly overtime, as well as overhead and rework expenses.

The American Automobile Association is another company that has made quality its trademark. Its members utilize AAA-certified repair facilities and lodgings because they have come to depend on AAA's recommendation as a guarantee of quality. To receive certification, an establishment must meet AAA's high standards and be inspected by field investigators. In addition, association members who use the services of affiliated establishments are asked to complete a "query card" at the time service work is completed. During one test period, 400,000 responses were collected; 96 percent said they were pleased with the quality of service, and 97 percent said that they would return to an AAA repair shop.

A key to quality, and a usually reliable indicator of quality, is a clean workplace. Hammond Berry, a furniture manufacturer, says: "A clean, orderly workplace promotes quality. I can almost sense the extent of a plant's quality level by just walking through and observing their housekeeping.

"Ever see a plant after it's been straightened up for annual inventory? I used to take pictures which were then used as 'the acceptable standard' for the rest of the year.''

A MULTI-FACETED APPROACH

Hewlett-Packard, a high-tech manufacturer, took steps to improve quality when it realized that as much as 25 percent of its manufacturing assets were tied up in "reactions" to quality problems. The lack of quality was raising production costs and product prices, so the company decided to take an aggressive, five-step approach to quality and achieved impressive results.

First, quality goals were identified, including the reduction of product failure rates by an ambitious 1,000 percent. Second, managers were trained in quality assurance techniques: doing it right the first time was the principal lesson. The third step was to train and motivate all employees by setting up more than 1,000 quality teams throughout the company and by reinforcing the quality message through newsletters, informal meetings, and formal training classes. A fourth step involved the installation of a computer system for tracking rework and parts failure, so that employees would have ready access to any information that would enable them to detect and remedy weaknesses that could lead to production faults.

As a final step, Hewlett-Packard asked its suppliers to establish similar quality goals and to set up their own quality assurance programs. The company knew that the reliability of its own products depended heavily on the reliability of components purchased from other companies.

In the end, Hewlett-Packard's results were outstanding. The service and repair of desk-top computers decreased 35 percent, while production time also dropped, resulting in lower costs and in some cases lower prices. (The cost of two of the company's oscilloscopes, for example, fell 30 percent.) As a result of its insistence on quality from suppliers, one vendor reduced chip failures to zero over a period of fifteen months, so parts no longer needed to be inspected as they came in. Finally, inventories were reduced over a three year period from 20.2 percent of sales to 15.5 percent. Translated into sales, Hewlett-Packard had saved $200 million on parts not tied up in inventory.

To be more competitive, you must be productive.
To be more productive, you must manage.
To manage more effectively, you must control.
To control consistently, you must measure.
To measure validly, you must define.
To define meaningfully, you must quantify.
—James Riggs, former Director
Oregon Productivity Center

5

MEASUREMENT:
Knowing How Productive You Are

Measuring everyone's productivity—including your own—is important because it enables you to evaluate the results of your efforts to improve your competitive position. The purpose of measurement is to know how you are doing and how well you are doing it, so every manager who seeks productivity improvement should find a way of measuring results. If you can feel a change, you can measure it.

The very notion of measurement, however, often stirs up a host of negative reactions. To those who must be evaluated, measurement can sometimes be a threatening experience. And to those who must do the evaluation, measurement can be both overwhelming and boring. So why does anyone ever measure? First, because measuring how successful you already are often generates even greater success, and secondly, because measurement simply does *not* have to be threatening, overwhelming, or even boring.

CONSENT OF THE GOVERNED

Any measurement of productivity is a lot more useful if it is developed with the assistance of those who are to be evaluated. Operating with "the consent of the governed" is as practical in the economic sphere as it is in the political arena. Every employee has a sense of how well he or she is doing, and every manager, likewise, has a feeling about the value of the people he manages. These personal assessments are expressed in the workplace quite frequently—but not always in a way that seems like a "measure."

Talking about these personal assessments is a first step in developing a useful measurement system. When a manager and an employee can agree on what they are trying to accomplish and how they can judge their success, they have developed a productivity measure. Sometimes just the process itself of talking about evaluation criteria will improve productivity, because a worker may find out for the first time what it is the manager really wants.

MEASURE FOR MEASURES

Even in the simplest of occupations, however, there is no single instrument that measures total productivity. Take a straight piecework job, for example, where a worker stamps out parts and is paid at a set rate for each unit produced. You might think that the best measure of productivity would be the number of pieces completed each hour, and that is certainly one good possibility. But other measures are also useful, especially when they can be related to production expenses. Counting the number of unacceptable pieces produced each hour will help incorporate scrap costs, for instance, while calculating the number of pieces produced weekly, instead of hourly, will give an indication of the rate of production over a sustained period of time.

One of the best illustrations of the many ways to measure productivity is our national pastime of baseball. Each year, record books are filled with measures of performance for each player: home runs per game, per inning, per season; batting averages; games played; runs batted in. The statistics are unending, and some of them may even seem excessive. But a great many of these ratings are useful measures in determining how much a player should be paid.

Developing measures to determine compensation is a continuing challenge, and not just in baseball. Prince Corporation, an auto parts manufacturer, recognizes that no one measure is sufficient, so it has developed a multimeasurement system to assess employee performance and to determine pay. Each employee at Prince is given a score of one to five in five key areas—attendance, quality, quantity, cooperation, and work rules—and hourly wages are determined on the basis of cumulative scores.

Measuring attendance is a lot easier than measuring quality, however. So all employees at Prince are asked to audit their own work using a standardized quality rating system. In addition, each worker's output goes through a series of computerized tests, whose results are posted daily. Both measures give employees an objective evaluation of the quality of their performance and tell them immediately which areas are subject to improvement.

MEASURING THE INTANGIBLE

It is always easier to measure the work performance of someone who produces a tangible product than it is to measure someone in the information or service industries. In fact, there are those who contend that there really is no meaningful way to measure the productivity of a lawyer, an accountant, a floor sweeper, a hotel clerk, or an author.

At a recent meeting of writers and reporters, for example, most of the participants agreed that while it is possible to measure the productivity of blue-collar workers, it is not possible to measure effectively the work of people who are concerned with "matters of the intellect." Their product, they said, could only be measured by counting words, and that did not take into consideration the quality of the work. For instance, one reporter had produced eighty-seven stories during the year with an average length of 400 words, while another reporter had produced only half as many of the same length.

But during further discussion, someone commented that it would be interesting to know how many hours each reporter spent on each story, how many stories received prime placement in newspapers and magazines (i.e., how many home runs per year), or how many retractions had to be made (i.e., number of strike outs). In the end, most of the participants concluded that although they could think of no comprehensive way to evaluate the overall productivity of reporters, a variety of useful measurements could be assembled.

No job category is beyond measurement or evaluation. But it is also important to remember that no single statistic that relates to worker effort should be regarded as an absolute measure of productivity. Numbers and averages cannot be equated with productivity *per se* in every instance. After all, how does one measure Lincoln's productivity with the Gettysburg Address?

Many modern Presidents, however, are frequently measured on the productivity of their speeches and in a number of different ways. Newspaper commentators provide instant assessments of how likely it is that the speech will produce its intended purpose, while the White House itself sets up phone banks to measure results: how many calls came in? how many were favorable? how many were unfavorable? Polls are also taken immediately after the speech to measure public reaction, and congressmen are grilled on whether the speech has convinced them to pass legislation. With today's sophisticated measurement tools, the productivity of the presidency is under continuous scrutiny.

Like editors and reporters, many educators also claim that their jobs are beyond useful productivity measurement. And the ongoing debate over whether teachers should receive merit pay is, in part, a productivity issue. The real question here is not whether teachers ought to be awarded merit pay, but whether any unbiased system can be devised to evaluate performance fairly.

But educational institutions have been using productivity measurement systems for many years, especially in schools of higher learning. Among the criteria that have been used for evaluation are the number of hours taught, the number of students in each class, the number of publications authored, membership on committees, and critiques of colleagues and students.

There are also a number of ways to measure a school's overall productivity, either by creating standardized tests or mandating statewide examinations just prior to graduation. The scores from these exams offer educators the opportunity to evaluate the change in a student's performance from year to year as a result of the time spent with a particular teacher or set of teachers. Managers who use the scores in hiring recent graduates have the opportunity to evaluate the effectiveness of that graduates' school system.

BEA Associates, a fund management firm, is one organization that has successfully grappled with the problem of how to measure the productivity of those whose work results in an intangible product. Each BEA fund manager's performance is measured monthly by the return on investment of the funds under his or her management, and portfolios are periodically reviewed for risk and diversification. Yearly performances are analyzed by a research unit that determines where value was added and by whom, and each fund manager is required to study the report and indicate in writing what each manager's compensation should be. Final results are collected and read aloud, but individual evaluators remain anonymous.

HIGH-TECH MEASURES

Today, computers make it possible to gather and compare productivity data at relatively low cost. But just because companies have the means to measure productivity does not mean that they will all do so. Some firms do not want to know how they are doing because they are reluctant to change their behavior, to be judged, or take the time to create truly accurate measurements.

General Foods is one corporation that has harnessed the power of the computer in an effort to achieve its primary objective: becoming the lowest-cost food producer in the markets it serves. To accomplish this feat, a sophisticated measurement system was developed called the Plantwide Productivity Measurement Program (PPMP). The PPMP is composed of individual Productivity Indexes (PI) devised for every facet of every product made by General Foods. Developed from standard cost accounting data, these indexes can be totaled up to produce an overall productivity index for each company product or plant. A base-year productivity index was computed by dividing total output by total input, and subsequent output/input calculations have been adjusted for inflation. Factors the company includes in measuring output are labor costs per unit of output and materials lost per unit of output. [Input factors include direct labor, indirect labor, purchased services and supplies, raw materials, energy, depreciation, property taxes, insurance, and cost of capital.] General Foods has found the PPMP to be extremely useful in identifying production inefficiencies and in arriving in cost reduction targets.

APPLES TO APPLES

Once you have developed an equitable system for measuring productivity, you will then have the ability to compare your current performance with past results, performance on one job with work performance for a related activity, one individual's performance with another's, or the performance in one unit or division with that of the rest. Comparing your organization's productivity with industry standards is also useful. Be sure not to overlook the benefits to be gained from comparing changes in productivity over time.

Continental Insurance, a domestic property and casualty company with forty branch offices throughout the U.S., uses a productivity measurement system called the Productivity Performance Index (PPI) to standardize branch expenses. Before instituting the PPI, the company had noticed that branch expenses varied widely from 3 to 13 percent of total premium income.

Three different measurements go into producing PPI. First, to evaluate staffing levels and to compare branch office efficiencies, a Productivity Indicator weighs transaction costs according to difficulty for each processing unit in each branch. Secondly, the ratio of transaction expenses to premium income is calculated to evaluate relative costs of processing. And finally, service timeliness is measured by figuring out the average number of days required to process different insurance instruments. When added together, these measurements produce an overall measure of productivity, cost, and effectiveness.

With the PPI pegged to a constant base index, Continental's branch managers can detect any changes in productivity at their locations, while the company can compare the performance of one branch to another and make recommendations on ways to cut costs for those branches performing less productively. And being able to measure productivity has increased productivity throughout the organization. In the first year of using the PPI, service levels at Continental rose 12.5 percent, branch expenses dropped 5 percent, and branch offices were able to reduce their staff by 20 percent through attrition and early retirement. Having seen the contribution productivity could make to profits and competitiveness, Continental began to examine additional alternatives for raising productivity further. The PPI concept has become part of the company culture rather than remaining a separate program.

A BAROMETER OF PROFITS

The ultimate measure of any company's productivity and competitiveness, however, is the bottom line, the net profit. It has become the ultimate symbol of how well a company is doing—and a reliable indicator of how long it will survive. Return on capital and percentage earnings on sales have become a mainstay of financial analysis. Even not-for-profit White House Conferences have come to appreciate them, for they too realize they cannot operate in the red for very long.

It is profits that make a company grow, and productivity growth is only a vehicle by which profits *can* grow. But without rising productivity, competitive position is likely to slip and profits are likely to fall. And because productivity contributes to profitability, its measure is also an early indicator of any changes that are likely to occur in net income.

So if you want to see your profits climb, make sure that your productivity is always going up. Productivity measures should be relatively simple, easy to compute, and readily available. After all, measurements are only as good as the use you can make of them.

The real art of management lies in the maximum utilization of ordinary men and women. Long-term success will go to those who know how to release the energy, zest, and hidden potential in us all.

—*John G. Quay*
Training and Development Journal
March 1968

6

PRODUCTIVE PEOPLE: Harnessing Your Most Important Resource

Successful managers may argue over the many different technologies and techniques for increasing corporate competitiveness, but there is one crucial point on which they all agree: it is people who make the difference. Large or small, all successful companies acknowledge the importance of their employees. "Recognize people as our most important asset," begins the Dana Corporation's statement of principles, and even the technological giant IBM credits people, not technology, with responsibility for its incredible rate of growth and record of excellence.

Recognizing the integral relationship between people and productivity, competitive edge, and profitability, means understanding that all employees are unique individuals. They are motivated and moved by values they hold to be important, and these values change from generation to generation. Your current employees are different from their parents and from any other other generation. Their educational backgrounds, desires, needs, and attitudes about work have changed, and the way they are managed needs to change accordingly.

Many traditional methods of management are not effective in motivating the current generation of workers. Even companies quick to adopt the latest technologies and manufacturing techniques are late in recognizing the new needs of their people. The result is often a company at odds with itself: a new breed of workers operating in a highly competitive environment, utilizing state-of-the-art technology, but managed by supervisors using the methods and styles of an older generation.

MOTIVATING THE NEW BREED

The competitive challenge for today's managers is to adapt their style to this new breed of workers and this changed environment. Managers must work to unleash the potential of each and every worker they supervise. A survey conducted by Robert Ranftl, director of managerial productivity for Hughes Aircraft Company, found that personal productivity has little to do, in fact, with IQ, schools attended, or course grades. What makes the critical difference in a worker's performance, the survey found, is the attitude and motivation of management that is transmitted downward. "Skilled, responsible, [motivating] management and superior productivity are inseparable," says Ranftl.

How do you motivate this new breed of workers and build positive competitive attitudes? According to Jerry McAdams, senior manager of Maritz, Inc., an employee benefits advisory firm based in Fenton, Missouri, you have to "create an organization where people share a sense of common fate, not an organization where people have a sense of controlled exchange—money for brawn and brain." And according to Barbard Nouveau, director of human resources for the Food Marketing Institute, that means letting people know about the organization in which they work. "They'll have more respect for their company and their job if they understand how the firm works—they might have good ideas as well. The old way of not letting employees in on the inner workings of a company is not valid anymore."

For John Manoogian, Ford Motor Company's director of quality assurance, an effective management style for today is one that also involves a good deal of listening. "Why should we reinvent the wheel when our employees already know how to get things rolling?" asks Manoogian. "Listening and responding to suggestions reduces obstacles to raising productivity, profitability, and competitiveness."

Involving workers in the decision-making process and recognizing them for their efforts is also critical. "Make people feel that they are part of the team," says Hoyt Parmer, president of Como Plastics. And according to Gene Kofke, Director of Human Resources at AT&T, "The one word that will have the greatest impact on labor-management relations and on productivity is recognition."

In short, treating people as you would like to be treated is the golden rule for modern management. Communicating, rewarding, listening, responding, delegating, and teaching are all key to reaping a bountiful return. And becoming more competitive depends on work force understanding of one important and basic principle: an improved competitive position through higher productivity helps everyone. The first job of management, therefore, is to communicate to workers that being more productive will make their company more competitive and that, in turn, will make their jobs and opportunities for success more secure.

Unfortunately, recent research suggests that managers have not been all that successful in getting this point across. A U.S. Chamber of Commerce study, in fact, indicates that only 9 percent of U.S. workers believe that productivity programs—or their company becoming more competitive—will benefit them personally.

So all managers need to convince themselves, first, and then their employees that productivity, competitiveness, and profitability are important to any worker who seeks to improve his or her economic status. Indeed, productivity improvement is the principal basis for increasing "real"—after inflation—income. When productivity declined in the U.S. in 1979, 1980, and 1982, for example, so did real incomes. And when inflation soared in 1979 and 1980, pay raises, in the end, just couldn't keep up, because higher salaries without higher productivity just meant higher prices. When more goods are produced and sold using the same amount of resources, however, then genuine economic gains are made, and there are ample dollars for bonuses and other rewards.

There is no one solution—no magic elixir or formula—for achieving increased people productivity. Success can be attained only through a multitude of strategies: by talking to your employees and letting them know what your goals and needs are; by listening to what your people say and letting them know their opinions are valued; by acting on employee suggestions and grievances; by seeking the cooperation of labor in creating innovative systems; and, finally, by recognizing and rewarding those who contribute to your success.

Productivity improvements cannot be harvested overnight. Companies that reap the benefits of improved productivity do so because of the long-term commitment they have made. Productivity programs "cost a bundle in time and a bundle in people effort," says Warren Braun, president of ComSonics. "But I tell you, they do work and they work beautifully." And Braun should know. Over the past five years, his company has generated a whopping 269-percent increase in sales, earning it a place on *Inc.* magazine's list of the 500 fastest-growing companies in America.

In the following two chapters, we will concentrate on innovative ways managers can use to help motivate their people to be more productive and competitive.

*Most people want to do a good job if they un-
derstand what it is that's expected of them, how
they relate to the whole, where the company is
going and how they are going to get there, and
how they fit into it.*
—*Donald Seibert, Former Chairman,*
J. C. Penney Company

7

COMMUNICATION:
Doing It Up and Down the Organization

No matter how simple it sounds or how often it is heard, it still is absolutely true: good communication is essential to improving productivity. The problem, however, is that most managers think they are adept at communicating or that they are already doing it. And in all too many cases, they are not. How can a manager start the communication process? First, quite simply, by telling employees what the company's goals and strategies are.

Employees base their actions on what they think management wants. But too often employee actions are based on incorrect guesses or gossip rather than on accurate information. Yet unless employees know where their company is headed and how it plans to get there, how can they be expected to take the same route or even go in the same direction?

"It's important for employees to know what the company is all about," emphasizes Don Gross, President of Certified Grocers of California. "You have to say it at the top level and mean it all the way down. Every employee has to know he is making a concrete contribution to a defined goal."

At Hughes Aircraft, the commitment to productivity is companywide and starts with the chairman and president. "We cross-pollinate productivity information throughout the company," explains Hughes productivity director Robert Ranftl. And once managers learned that communication was important to the company, they started sharing ideas across the board.

Several years ago, for example, Hughes made the decision to invest heavily in capital improvement. "We took the initiative and put out a brochure, *A Commitment to Productivity*, and sent it to all 70,000 employees," says Ranftl. "The brochure spelled out our $1 billion commitment to new technology, and told the employees dollar by dollar how the money would be spent. We solicited their involvement and their commitment to improved productivity. And of greatest importance, we looked to our managers themselves as a key to this entire process. We're trying to develop not only an awareness and an understanding of productivity, but a dedicated commitment to it on the part of our management team."

At ComSonics, a manufacturer and maintainer of cable TV broadcast equipment, the company takes a participatory approach to achieving corporate goals. A clear set of objectives is established for the company as a whole and for each division and individual. And once these objectives are communicated, employees may accomplish them using whatever methods they see fit.

Communicating goals is just the start of the process, however. Employees also need to know about strategies, budgets, productive ideas, compensation plans, board members, promotions, retirements, awards, company history, and competitor efforts. In short, employees need to know what management knows, information that will provide a basis for achieving common objectives and reinforcing their commitment to the company's success.

Sharing with employees financial data that was previously held confidential is a strategy recently adopted by Como Plastics. When C.W. Jackson purchased the company in 1980, he brought with him a "people oriented" management approach that relies heavily on face-to-face meetings. Now, managers meet regularly with production personnel and staff to discuss each month's financial figures.

In addition, Jackson and Hoyt Parmer, the company president, hold a breakfast meeting with twelve or thirteen employees each month where the agenda is wide open: everything from production techniques and new product lines to retirement benefits and profits are discussed. And this approach seems to have paid off handsomely. Sales at Como Plastics jumped from $8 million to $17 million in these years, and profits increased by a whopping 800 percent.

But communication means not only providing information about the company, it also means talking to employees about issues that are usually not aired publicly—personnel matters, for example, or competitive strategies. For the most part, employees can be trusted to keep this information confidential when told the reasons it is not for public consumption.

LISTEN UP!

Good communication is a two-way street. Information has to be communicated up and down the line. That is why listening is the second most important aspect of good communication, even though most managers have been better trained to "tell" than to listen. The best problem solver is frequently the manager who listens to the answer instead of talking through it.

Bad news never gets better with age, and it is important that managers hear about problems as soon as they occur. In most organizations, however, it is very difficult to communicate disappointments. Telling your boss bad news is sometimes the hardest of all. If managers expect to be tipped off to impending problems or disasters, they must develop a reputation for reacting well to the information they receive, and must thank the messenger who delivers it.

Teaching managers to listen sometimes requires an effort of considerable magnitude. But those managers who learn the trick have found, like the managers at the Ford Motor Company, that their employees can solve a good number of their productivity problems for them.

For many years Ford strived to improve the way its cars were assembled, but it was common practice, explains Chairman Philip Caldwell, to "kick the man downstream who couldn't put the parts together because the parts really weren't designed properly. Eventually we realized that the assemblers might have something to contribute [to solving] the problem." Today, prototype vehicles are taken to the plants where they are to be assembled, and line workers are given the chance to run the process and make suggestions. The benefits are many: not only does Ford solve its design problems before they can sabotage the assembly process, but workers feel good about their jobs because their suggestions are taken seriously. And the resulting increase in productivity benefits both workers and management.

"Our employees protect our blind side," explains a manager at a midwestern manufacturing plant. "Who will ask 'what if'? We rely on our own people, not our competitors or apple polishers, to do that for us."

"It makes sense to value the opinions of employees," says another manager we talked to. "Most employees have well organized, prosperous lives outside the office, and they thrive in interactive collaborative environments. By sharing information and decision making, you can tap this outside resource for use inside the organization."

Sometimes, however, managers are inhibited from communicating and listening because they do not know how to solicit employee suggestions while maintaining control at the same time. Workers need to feel that their opinions count, yet managers need to feel that they are still in charge. "You have to realize that you're not really installing a democracy," explains Bob Cowie, senior vice president of Dana, "you still have to run the plant. (Employees) *want* you to run the plant, but they want to be involved in it, too."

COMMUNICATION TECHNIQUES: HOW AND WHEN TO TALK

Many managers are reluctant to communicate because they feel it takes time away from more "productive" activities. But if employees are to take their commitment seriously, the company has to provide opportunities for communication on its own time. This sends the message to employees that the company cares enough to pay them while they talk and listen. At Dana, the entire plant is shut down when employees are brought together for twenty or thirty minutes to discuss sales, profits, and production problems.

Besides using company time, however, a manager can also communicate during time that belongs strictly to the employee, such as the few minutes before and after work, lunch periods, or even time at home. Generally, a mix of company time and personal time works best. And once employees come to realize how regular and systematic exchanges can benefit them, they are much more willing to give up personal time.

Many communication techniques, such as formal meetings, informal "walk-abouts," open houses, plant visits, and memos, can be incorporated into a manager's daily routine, while other communication techniques require more time and planning. A few of these are described below.

Easy Listening

When one communicates with employees, try to incorporate a personal touch. Individual letters to an employee's home, plant visits by a manager, or random walks about the office—all provide the kind of contact that lets employees know there is a "face" to management.

What is more, many of these personal encounters provide employees with the opportunity to discuss how to improve their own productivity, how they view the company's policies, and how they think the workplace can become more enjoyable or more efficient.

Open Houses

Inviting employees to "stop by" is always a useful communication tool. All executives should let their people know that they are available at certain times each week or month and that any individual is also welcome to set up a special appointment just to talk. For many employees, merely *knowing* that they have access to the "top brass" is important: it allows them to feel that they have a place to go, if necessary, to let off steam or just be heard.

At IBM, employees know that the doors of management are always open to listen to complaints. In fact, every manager's performance evaluation at IBM includes an appraisal of how they handle employee complaints. If employees feel that they have not been given a fair hearing, they can appeal to a higher level. Though few complaints have had to go through many successive management levels, some have reached the chairman's desk.

As with other communication tools, however, control and coordination of the open-door policy is necessary, including setting time limits.

Memos and Minutes

Posting the minutes of a senior management meeting or circulating a management memo or other work document is another effective communication technique that gives authenticity to information. For who doesn't appreciate getting the story firsthand and hot off the press? Everyone likes to be part of the "in crowd," and disseminating information in this way helps to build team spirit.

Group Approaches

Work groups or teams are more formal communication tools, but they can provide real benefits, too: they not only create vehicles for employee participation, they facilitate problem solving as well. By volunteering for these groups, employees can find out what on-the-job participation really means, while providing effective remedies to the perennial "there's got to be a better way" dilemma.

Work groups can take any number of forms, but they function best when specific tasks or productivity objectives are set, such as reducing quality defects in an assembly line. Quality circle work teams are usually the most effective in assimilating different viewpoints to find a common solution to a specific set of problems.

Champion International, a manufacturer of wood building materials and paper products, has worked with the American Productivity Center to develop quality circle work teams. When a specific problem is identified in one of the company's mills, for example, an area supervisor begins putting together a team by recruiting eight to ten interested managers and line employees. Normally, a first-line supervisor serves as the team leader, while quality circle coordinators and facilitators lead the group through problem identification and solution techniques.

Once operational, a team meets at least once a month to discuss the nature and cause of the problem in question and to come up with alternative solutions. And when all the team members have agreed on a final solution to the problem, a presentation is made to the area supervisor, who then has to decide whether or not to take the recommended action. After its work on one project is completed, the team has the option of remaining together to brainstorm solutions for other problems.

Twenty-three quality circle teams have been formed at Champion, which estimates that they saved the company $1 million at the Pasadena Mill and $7 million overall in the paper division during their first year. And along with these cost savings, of course, have come increased job satisfaction, higher morale, and significant productivity improvements.

Quality circles are also a cornerstone of management at Donnelly Mirrors, a Michigan manufacturer of mirrors and modular windows for the auto industry. Every one of Donnelly's more than 1,000 employees, including the president, is a member of at least one quality circle, which meets regularly to set goals and solve problems. "In general," says one of the company's senior managers, "they have not disappointed us, but continue to find new and creative ways to meet the needs of our demanding markets." Over a recent seven-year period, Donnelly's return on investment was 220 percent, and company officials credit half the company's productivity improvement to this quality circle approach.

While the success of quality circles depends largely on consensus and compromise, "organized listening groups," on the other hand, thrive on diversity. The goal of these work groups is called "option decision making"—that is, identifying various viable alternatives and then evaluating their potential for success or failure. To start the organized listening process, a group of employees at various levels is given a company problem to brainstorm solutions: How do we check in crowds faster at the hotel front desk? How do we cut down on absenteeism? What is the highest priority for our new computer? Each of the various solutions presented will often have its own supporters within the group. Variety—not unanimity—is the objective of this exercise.

A variation of this group technique is called "competitive organized listening." Here key executives, usually from the middle management ranks and representing all major parts of the organization, are divided into teams. Each team is presented with the same problem and competes with the others by developing its own solutions. This approach has the advantage of involving a greater number of employees in the decision-making process, and the competitive angle provides additional incentives to participate.

COMMUNICATION EQUALS INNOVATION

Once you open up the communication process, you will probably find that your employees will be better able to solve some very sticky problems. The Westinghouse Nuclear Technology Division (NTD), the Great Salt Lake Minerals & Chemical Corporation, and The Travelers Insurance Company have improved communications resulting in better working conditions, increased productivity, and a sharper competitive edge.

Westinghouse NTD recognized that the primary nature of its business was changing from that of power plant design to engineering product application. This meant that its work force would also have to change, because the company no longer needed its high concentration of superstar professionals—3.5 engineers for every technician.

To develop a productivity plan that could estimate future staffing requirements, NTD's management went to employees and said, "You know our work is changing. Tell us what skills are needed to do your job." Employees were asked to calculate the time they spent on each task and to rate the importance of the tasks they performed in three areas: production, service, and R&D. Five different engineering skill levels were then established based on the relative amount of time required to perform each task.

The survey revealed that 20 to 30 percent of the activities performed by senior engineers could actually be handled by technicians and because of seasonal mass hirings, an enormous amount of time was being spent in on-the-job training. In addition, engineers told management that they did not like doing work that was not really challenging them.

As a result of a concentrated follow-up effort to restructure jobs and establish new hiring requirements, the company was able to shift much of the routine work previously performed by engineers, lowering the ratio of professionals to technicians to 2.7:1. This was accomplished without layoffs, by moving some senior engineers to other divisions and not replacing others about to retire. Hiring practices were also changed to alleviate the training burden. New recruits were trained throughout the year, rather than bringing them on board in seasonal "bunches."

In the end, the MPWR—Matching People and Work Requirements—project benefited both the company and its employees. During each of the first two years, NTD achieved an eight-percent payroll savings, indicating that the eight-percent savings would be a recurring annual benefit. In addition, job satisfaction has increased; employees are both more productive and more interested in their work. Most importantly, however, a long-term human resource planning mechanism has been put in place, helping to ensure that in the future the right people will be hired for the right job.

At the Great Salt Lake Minerals and Chemicals Corporation, sleeping on the job was a real problem for workers on rotating shifts. In fact, one-third of the workers at the $37-million-a-year solar pond system reported that they could not make it through their eight-hour shift without a nap.

With the help of the Center for Design of Industrial Schedules and Harvard University, the company asked employees to help diagnose and cure the problem.

It soon became clear that by changing shifts every seven days and rotating forward, employees were interrupting their internal body clocks, or what scientists would call their "circadian cycles." So the company decided to experiment to accommodate this natural rhythm and found that when workers rotated to a later shift instead of the earlier one, fatigue decreased. It also discovered that by scheduling shift changes every twenty-one days instead of seven, further improvements could be seen in a worker's ability to adjust.

With the adoption of these simple shift changes, Great Salt Lake's "sleep problem" was virtually solved. Employees were not only more awake, they were more productive, more competitive, and happier. There was a 70 percent decrease in scheduling complaints, as well as a significant decline in employee turnover, absenteeism, and family problems. And in the first year of implementing the new schedules, productivity increased twenty percent. "Four years ago," Operations Manager Preston Richey points out, "our goal was 1,000 tons of potash per day, but we were able to achieve an average of 1,500 tons per day with the same work force. Although the potash operations were curtailed due to flooding of the pond system, all other operating areas continued in 1987 to show about 3% to 7% improvement and none has shown a loss.

At The Travelers companies, it was also found that satisfying basic employee needs can rebound to the company's advantage. When employees over fifty-five were asked about their retirement plans, it was discovered that almost 70 percent of the company's pre-retirement work force was interested in some form of continuing employment after sixty-five and that over half were interested in working for Travelers on a part-time basis.

The response of those already retired was even more telling. Former employee Evelyn Smith's comments were typical: "During my first year of retirement, I did just what you would expect—travel, lunches, needlepoint. But it wasn't enough for me. I felt I needed to be on a schedule for structure as well as for stimulation." In short, she wanted to go back to work.

Travelers had a problem, too. It often needed temporary and part-time workers in its claims department, but the temporaries that were hired had little previous experience with the job and little interest in becoming proficient at it. Then Travelers realized that by addressing the concerns of its older workers, it could solve its own problems as well.

The company decided to develop job options for older workers and retirees. First, it eliminated mandatory retirement, then it identified jobs that could be filled efficiently with qualified retirees. Third, a job sharing scheme was devised as an alternative to part-time employment. Finally, the Travelers Board of Directors agreed to double the number of hours a retiree could work without losing pension benefits, and set up a job bank at the Hartford headquarters to match retired people with available positions.

Travelers found that by listening to employee concerns, it could become more productive, more competitive, and more profitable. Its new program has been well received. Older workers have a greater sense of peace about their transition into retirement, and corporate morale has improved: workers are now convinced that Travelers really cares about its people. Travelers meets 60 percent of its temporary employment needs by hiring retirees and estimates that it saves $1 million annually by not using more costly temporary employment agencies.

LABOR PAINS

Communicating directly with employees can sometimes be difficult, especially when there is a third party—the union—to be considered.

Many managers view unions as obstacles to getting their job done. They feel thwarted by union work rules, which they see as a barrier to improving productivity. By the same token, many union leaders tend to view management simply as a potential exploiter of their rank and file.

How do you get heretofore mortal enemies to realize that their successes are ultimately interdependent? By convincing them that joint initiatives to create a competitive, successful company benefit *both* labor and management. Unfortunately, however, getting labor and management to cooperate in joint efforts that will reap rewards down the road is not so easy.

Managers can begin by following the same policy of communicating that we outlined above. That means providing information directly to union representatives as well as to employees. Given the long tradition of collective bargaining in this country, things may be a bit difficult at first, but the goal of cooperation may be reached once everyone realizes that the alternative is to become an unprofitable company with a poor chance of survival.

Richard Mantia, an official with the St. Louis Building and Construction Trades Council, is one far-sighted union representative who recognizes the interdependence of labor and management. He looks at the situation from the bottom line: "If we're going to keep the AFL-CIO alive, we have to keep the AFL-CIO contractors in business. You have to begin [the joint initiative process] by taking the first step."

In the seventies, St. Louis had a notorious reputation as a particularly difficult trade union city. Strikes closed construction sites several times a month and businesses began to defer expansion because of the tense climate. Eventually, however, union and construction industry leaders both realized that, in order to survive, they would have to change.

To break the impasse, leaders of the Building and Construction Trades Council sat down with the Associated General Contractors, and with the aid of architects, engineers, and material suppliers, a "memorandum of understanding" called PRIDE—Productivity and Responsibility Increase Development and Employment—was drawn up. As its name implied, its goal was to increase construction productivity, development, and employment in the St. Louis area. In order to do so, each party had to agree to compromise. The unions eased work rules, eliminated featherbedding, banned jurisdictional strikes, and strengthened on-site management control. In return for a no-picket-line pledge during contract strikes, management agreed to non-binding arbitration and contractors agreed to hire only union labor.

Having reached an initial understanding about how to improve the declining labor-management climate, PRIDE then went on to focus on prevention. The future was addressed at monthly meetings and efforts were made to solve problems before they became serious obstacles to productivity.

Because of PRIDE, construction in the St. Louis area quickly went from bust to boom. Trade union members became fully employed, with 98 percent of commercial-industrial and 96 percent of residential construction built by AFL-CIO labor. Moreover, projects were completed on time and under budget.

PRIDE's example has been successfully copied in at least ten other cities around the country. Included among them are the MOST program (Management and Organized Labor Sticking Together) in Columbus, Ohio, the PEP project (Planning Economic Progress) in Beaumont, Texas, and the UNION JACK in Denver, Colorado.

To keep communication between management and labor open and flowing, however, a third party is sometimes required. Phillip Ray, former director of the Joint Labor Management Committee (JLMC) of the Retail Foods Industry, believes that "a third party can play a very valuable role in being a facilitator between the two sides—and in making sure they're moving in some direction rather than just stalling."

The JLMC serves just this purpose. It convenes meetings for labor and management groups to talk about productivity issues, and serves as a clearinghouse for communication between the two sides. Composed of representatives from the three largest unions in the retail food industry, thirteen supermarket companies, and their trade association, the JLMC assumes a wide variety of responsibilities: monitoring and improving collective bargaining negotiations, preventing unnecessary strikes, promoting long-range industry stability, and encouraging open and high-level communication on industry issues.

The JLMC has had some impressive results in dealing with productivity problems, especially in influencing Occupations Safety and Health Administration (OSHA) regulations as they affect supermarket butchering. In the seventies, OSHA was still applying slaughterhouse standards for meat butchering to retail food store deli departments, even though procedures for wholesale and retail meat operations were quite different. Rather than engaging in a hostile court battle to change OSHA regulations, however, JLMC simply collected data and ironed out a labor-management agreement for modifying meat cutting standards for grocery stores that were later adopted by OSHA.

Not only did the modifications remove obstacles to productivity in grocery meat departments, it also saved labor, management, and government from having to engage in a lengthy, costly, and adversarial regulatory proceedings.

COMMUNITY TIES

Often good and on-going communication between labor, management and the community can be the basis for a revitalization of local enterprises. Industry, labor, and management are not the only ones who benefit from working together by talking together. Declining industries and companies can have a serious and detrimental impact on the areas in which they are located. After all, when a company lays off employees because of decreased sales, there is a corresponding general decline in income throughout the community.

Most communities that have been hit hard by the negative effects of troubled companies now realize that they, too, can help by banding together with labor and management to meet the economic challenge, whatever its source—foreign competition, changing market requirements, or the increasing obsolescence of U.S. industrial products. City and local governments all across the country are taking concrete steps to stimulate business opportunities by providing tax relief, changing zoning laws or building codes, and working with industry to provide educational training opportunities for workers. In most cases, government can do a lot more than just lend its influence, prestige, and support to a revitalization effort.

A united effort in Cleveland, Ohio, provides a good example of how business, labor, and community leaders revitalized a decaying business community and a bankrupt city. A task force of Cleveland's foremost business, municipal, and civic leaders came together to take a hard look at the city's problems, and according to Ruben Mettler, chairman of TRW Inc. and a leading member of the joint effort, the task force concluded that the basic issue that had to be addressed was the erosion of the community's competitive spirit. Once these leaders committed themselves to competing with foreign and domestic companies, however, the task force was able to chart a steady course for improving productivity and profitability.

The transition from bankruptcy to economic renaissance in Cleveland was brought about largely by the determination to face the facts directly and by making a formal commitment to becoming more competitive.

A SHARED DESTINY

There is an old saying that the "credit for doing a good job is one of the few things that can be multiplied by being divided." This certainly has been the case in the companies described above where the generous efforts put into labor-management initiatives have paid off handsomely.

Information is power and sharing information is a prerequisite for having a common basis of understanding. A common knowledge of the facts is essential to a cooperative effort. Communicate the facts first and then work on the problem.

Dr. Barbara Scott of the Boeing Military Airplane Company, however, believes that the central issue regarding how labor and management work together "is not cooperation . . . [but] shared power." The crux of the matter, then, is determining how this power will be shared. From the many case studies we have analyzed, it seems that those who have managed to carve a successful split seem to have done so on the basis of these guidelines:

1. Recognize that unless competitive position is improved through increased productivity, the jobs of all participants—labor and management alike—are in jeopardy.

2. Respect the ability of both sides to bring useful information and resources to the resolution of productivity problems.

3. Foster the development of a mutual interest by providing fair compensation and job security for labor and profits for the company.

4. Commit formally, in writing, to both long-range and short-range planning.

5. View technological change as both inevitable and desirable, and be willing to meet any hardships that may arise as a result of it.

6. Finally, keep frank and open discussions going at the highest levels, without publicity and public posturing, and with all relevant facts available to everyone concerned.

Employees must share in productivity gains.
—Michael McKay, Partner
Arthur Young & Company

8

REWARDS:
Recognizing Outstanding Competitors

Excellence deserves its reward. And companies that go out of their way to let employees know how valuable they are usually find mediocrity to be the exception among their work force, while companies that pay regardless of performance usually find mediocrity to be the norm.

There are many ways—both monetary and nonmonetary—to recognize outstanding performance. Monetary rewards, for example, come in a variety of forms: (1) pay-for-performance, in which each worker's compensation is based on his or her individual accomplishments; (2) pay-for-group-results, where the earnings of a single division or company are used to determine the compensation of the workers in it; (3) employee ownership plans, in which employees are rewarded through ESOPs, stock options, or stock bonuses; and (4) pay-for-skills programs, in which a worker's pay is based on the number of new skills that he or she has mastered.

Nonmonetary rewards can also work to increase productivity and competitiveness. They include: (1) employment security; (2) greater employee involvement in decision making; (3) giving employees increased responsibility for superior performance; and (4) sharing company information that was once considered confidential.

Just about anything you can do to recognize the superior performance of an individual will work to reinforce that person's contribution and extra effort. But rewards work best when they are specially tailored to the needs of your company and its employees. One of America's strengths, after all, is its heritage of individuality; no two companies have the same people or even the same characteristics. So whether you decide to set up an ESOP, bonus system, or pay-for-performance program, remember that it will always need to be adapted to your special work environment. Indeed, some companies have as many incentive plans as they have separate units and divisions.

REWARDS THAT WORK

To be successful, any reward system must contain several important "ingredients." Money is necessarily one of them, but there are many other ways to show a company's appreciation. The standards for determining who is to be rewarded are important and should be universally recognized as objective and fair. Employees should know how they will be measured, and the criteria used should be widely publicized—in the company newsletter, for example, or even at an award banquet. The rewards must also be something employees really want and should be bestowed promptly. Any delay may actually be counterproductive if employees lose sight of the connection between their performance and their reward.

How do you know what reward will motivate employees best? Just ask them! That is exactly what Certified Grocers did and found out to its surprise that it is *not* always money first. When the company set up employee-management groups to improve productivity in three key areas—warehouse operations, accounting, and data processing—the warehouse group boldly recommended a nonmonetary reward system: more time off for above-average performance. With the approval of the company's labor unions, Certified developed a performance standard based on an engineering analysis of the amount of work that could reasonably be expected in any job and in any given period of time. Whenever an employee's production now exceeds that standard, that person receives a bonus of paid time-off or, if the employee prefers, the monetary equivalent of one-half the time off.

Only a year after installing its new bonus plan, Certified found that its productivity was up more than 15 percent, and that the company had saved more that $2 million in payroll costs.

Not all reward systems start off with a bang, however. At ComSonics, what is now considered a highly successful employee stock ownership program had a very shaky beginning. "After the first year," explains President Warren Braun, "I thought I had a disaster on my hands. It was as if our people had been handed a stone rather than tools to work for greater profits." One of the reasons the ESOP was failing was that employees did not understand what it was or how it benefited them. Since they did not know how to read company financial statements or interpret stock prices, they could not easily evaluate the worth of their ownership. So instead of raising enthusiasm, the ESOP only helped to generate further dissatisfaction and anxiety.

The ultimate success of the plan was due in large part to an all-out communications effort that provided employees with the kinds of information they needed to understand the system. ComSonics hired a consultant to brief everyone on the concept of entrepreneurial risk and how they can share in the success of the organization. Eventually, employees were also taught how to monitor the finances of the company—of which they now own 40 percent.

THE INDIVIDUAL OR GROUP APPROACH

Outstanding work performance can be rewarded either individually or in groups, but either way, there must be a direct correlation between the work performed and the reward. At Prince Corporation in Holland, Michigan, each of the auto parts manufacturer's 1,000 employees is rewarded individually, with compensation tied to five measurable standards: quantity, quality, work rules, cooperation, and attendance. Though each employee functions as part of a team and relies on the performance of other team members, individual pay is based solely on individual performance. This approach has earned Prince top quality ratings from each of the major automakers.

The Potlatch Corporation, on the other hand, a billion-dollar producer of wood products, links compensation to group productivity. With the help of a consulting engineer and with union cooperation, the company developed an hours standard for the fabrication and packaging of 1,000 feet of paneling, and when employees work more efficiently, a bonus is paid. If the paneling is produced with a 10 percent savings in hours, for example, the company pays a 10 percent bonus to all line workers. Managers, clerical workers, and janitors, however, are excluded from the bonus system, which is based on a two-week moving production average.

Using this approach, productivity improvement at Potlatch has averaged 5 to 7 percent a year and bonuses 5 to 8 percent, while teamwork and product quality standards have remained strong. Installing the plan took Potlatch six to seven months from conception to implementation, at a cost of about $17,000, but the resulting increases in productivity and profits have more than offset the initial outlay of time and money.

At Lincoln Electric, a welding equipment manufacturer, individual and group incentives are combined. Wherever possible, jobs are paid on a piecework basis, so that individual accomplishments and efficiencies can be rewarded. But employees also receive year-end bonuses based on company profits, so everyone has an incentive to increase the corporate profit pie as well. Lincoln Electric has thrived in this environment—continuing operations while others in the industry have had to close down—and so have its employees. In one year alone, individual bonuses averaged more than $15,000!

All three types of incentive systems have the potential to increase productivity and competitiveness. Individual reward systems motivate workers to succeed for the good of the company because they benefit employees directly, while group systems help foster cooperation and teamwork, and combined systems can work to double the rewards.

But reward systems also work whether they are simple or complex. What *is* important is that they meet your objectives. Lowe's pay-for-profit plan, for example, involves employee participation, heavy committee work, and constant monitoring; but the cash bonus plan adopted by Como Plastics is much less complicated. There, bonuses are paid out when a set goal is reached—an 8-percent pre-tax profit, for example. If the projected goal is not met, there is no bonus. Simple or complex, however, what the plans at Lowe's and Como Plastics both have in common is that they work effectively in meeting company goals.

PAY-FOR-PERFORMANCE

Many employee surveys seem to indicate that money alone is not the best motivator. But it may rank higher than many people really care to admit to others—or to themselves. Monetary compensation gives employees choices: to splurge on a trip to Europe, to pay for further education, or to save for a rainy day. In practice, it appears that good old-fashioned cash is as effective as any reward that has yet been invented.

Paying cash rewards for performance is still a proven way for a company to increase its productivity and to gain or maintain the competitive edge in the marketplace. One form it may take is called "gainsharing," a tried-and-true system of motivating and rewarding employees either individually or in groups. In gainsharing, employees are told in advance what financial rewards they will receive if certain production or profit goals are met. Profit-sharing plans like "Improshare," "Scanlon," and "Rucker" are all popular forms of gainsharing. Each may take a different approach, but they are all based on the same principle: allowing workers to share the financial benefits of their company's increased profitability.

Most pay-for-performance programs base rewards on performance for a specific and predetermined period of time—a week, a month, or a fiscal year. In general, the more frequent the payout, the stronger the connection employees make between these benefits and their performance. And this connection is reinforced even further when rewards are paid as promised and on schedule.

Improshare (*Im*proved *Pro*ductivity through *Shar*ing) focuses on increasing productivity by lowering labor costs. And these reduced costs provide increased profits out of which bonuses are paid to employees. For example, were an automobile factory using Improshare to produce 50 more cars in a given month with the same amount of labor, a percentage of the labor savings from that increased production would be shared with all the factory's workers.

Scanlon plans are aimed at reducing labor costs. Whenever labor costs per dollar of sales fall below a certain average, a portion of the resulting savings is paid out as employee bonuses. The key to the Scanlon plan is that labor benefits from reducing its cost per dollar of sales, no matter what happens to other production costs. The employer gains by having a better competitive cost position, which usually leads to bigger sales and better profits.

Rucker plans are somewhat different, in that they share profits based on value that has been additional to the production process. This "value added" is computed by subtracting the cost of materials and supplies used in the production process from total sales receipts. Whenever value added rises without a corresponding rise in labor costs, there are additional Rucker revenues to be paid as bonuses (usually monthly) to employees.

Motorola, a manufacturer of consumer and commercial electronic products, takes the team approach to bonuses with its Participative Management Plan (PMP). Every Motorola employee is a member of a team, and each team is given certain performance goals by a PMP steering committee. For employees involved directly in manufacturing, team goals usually focus on cost, quality, delivery, inventory, housekeeping, and safety standards, while managers, supervisors, and other workers engaged in support positions have goals that emphasize strategic and human resource issues. To qualify for a bonus, a team must meet its goals and its pre-tax profit target. A proportion of the additional profit earned is then paid out in bonuses, with each member's bonus based on his or her salary's share of the team's total payroll.

The team approach is being seen by more and more companies as an opportunity to build a competitive spirit. In wage talks with the United Auto Workers (UAW), General Motors proposed that compensation be tied to productivity performance in its individual plants, thereby eliminating across-the-board pay raises for all workers regardless of the profitability of their particular division, plant, or line. Although the UAW objected to the proposal, saying that it threatens the union's ability to negotiate for all employees, such programs are likely to win out in the future.

For instance, the U.S. Air Force instituted an experimental program at Mc-Clellan Air Force Base in California that will tie the pay of 2,000 blue-collar workers to team performance. The workers' union, the American Federation of Government Employees, approves in theory of the concept of splitting the benefits of higher quality and higher output. The employees can expect better wages and greater job security, while the employer—Uncle Sam—can expect to get a better job done at a lower cost.

EMPLOYEES AS OWNERS

"Employee ownership plans," says Lowe's Chairman Robert Strickland, "are the most dynamic and most flexible gainsharing plans. They combine two very powerful forces: economics and human nature. When done correctly, they are seedbeds for motivation and productivity."

When workers become owners, they take a new interest in the health of their firm and usually do a better job. They think about what is good for the long-term future of the company, not just what seems attractive for tomorrow. Chrysler is a dramatic example of how making employees owners can help turn around a company in trouble, as is Lowe's chain of retail building supply stores.

"In the late 50s and early 60s," explains Strickland, "there were at least five companies in the sunbelt just like ours—same geography, same business, different management, of course, but not bad management. Three of the companies didn't make it on their own and sold out. The fourth company, which is about one-fourth our size, has just adopted an ESOP." Since adopting its own employee ownership plan in the late 1950s, Lowe's has grown from six stores to 205 in nineteen states, and its sales volume increased fifty times over. By 1983, Lowe's sales-per-employee figures were three times the average for the big three retailers (Sears, K-Mart and J.C. Penney), all non-employee-owned businesses.

Most importantly, Lowe's has found that employee ownership is a powerful motivator for those groups that are often the most difficult to motivate—young middle managers and low-income, blue-collar workers. "Now our aggressive young store managers check on their wealth every weekday by looking up Lowe's in the New York Stock Exchange listings," says Strickland. Blue-collar workers are motivated by the possibility of retiring with a big nest egg. An example: One Lowe's employee, who never earned more than $125 a week, was able to retire with $600,000 worth of Lowe's stock.

Employee ownership plans do more than just make employees rich, however; they also make corporations rich. One reason is that when employees are owners, they are more motivated to look for inefficiencies and bottlenecks— and to find out how to eliminate them.

Another reason is that employee stock ownership plans have been approved by the Internal Revenue Service to receive special tax treatment. That is because an ESOP is basically a trust fund in which shares of company stock are purchased with cash contributed from the company for the benefit of employees. Typically, the stock is held in the ESOP until an employee's retirement or termination (depending on vesting provisions). The employee acquires ownership of the employer's contribution, but pays no tax on it until it is actually withdrawn. These contributions are usually made when specific financial goals are achieved.

Ten years ago, few companies could see the benefits of employee stock ownership programs because the concept itself was so foreign to the traditional owner-employee relationship. During the last decade, however, the popularity of ESOP's has grown, and more than 4,000 plans are now in place. In addition, another 4,000 companies have alternative forms of stock bonus and employee ownership programs.

According to the National Center for Employee Ownership, ESOPs have clearly had a positive impact on productivity and competitiveness. After examining forty-five companies that used ESOPs over a ten-year period, the center reported that sales in companies with ESOPs grew about five-and-a-half percent a year faster than their non-ESOP competitors.

Until 1987, an employer could receive a tax credit for the value of stock contributed to certain stock ownership plans known as PAYSOPS, which were built around payroll-based contributions. This is no longer the case, however. The 1986 tax law eliminated PAYSOPs, which has further enhanced the attractiveness of ESOPs.

PROFIT SHARING PLANS

Employers can also receive special tax treatment by making contributions to profit sharing plans in the name of their employees. These contributions can amount to as much as 15 percent of wages paid during the year, but are not taxable to the employee until the funds are withdrawn, usually at retirement when tax rates are lower. Employees can also match the employer's contribution, and though their matching contributions must be made with after-tax dollars, the fund's earnings are not taxable until they are withdrawn. Instead of being taxed when income is at its peak, the employee's share of profits is put to work on a tax-deferred basis.

The incentive to work harder in a company with a profit sharing plan is simple: Since the plan gets funded with company profits, the higher the profits, the larger the funding—up to the limit allowed by law.

STOCK OPTIONS AND BONUSES

The IRS does not treat employee stock option and stock bonus plans as favorably as ESOPs, but these plans also represent valuable opportunities to reward employees at reduced costs to the company. More importantly, they make employees part-owners in the enterprise, which increase their level of interest in the long-term success of the organization.

Simply put, stock bonus programs substitute company stock for cash bonuses. This type of bonus program is especially attractive when a company is trying to conserve cash for faster future growth. And the company also receives a tax deduction for the total value of the stock that is awarded during any one year.

A stock option program provides benefits similar to a stock bonus plan, but instead of transferring stock to an employee immediately, it gives the employee the option of purchasing a certain amount of stock at some time in the future—but at a price that is set at the time the option is granted. This motivates the employee to work harder so that the market value of the company's stock will rise and the option price will become an even greater bargain.

DISCRETIONARY CASH BONUSES

Unlike gainsharing plans, where monetary rewards are paid when certain production or profit goals are met, some cash bonuses are paid at the discretion of a manager simply to reward an employee for a good idea, for instance, or for overall superior performance. And unlike profit sharing plans, these bonuses tend to be tied to individual base salaries rather than to unit or company profits. While discretionary cash bonuses are common in many small companies, they are often difficult to use where large numbers of employees are involved.

PAY-FOR-SKILLS

Rewarding employees for acquiring new skills and knowledge is another method that has also proven effective in boosting motivation and productivity. Such programs encourage employees to extend the limits of their capabilities, and in so doing, they usually provide increased labor value to their company. Pay-for-skills programs can help solve a multitude of management problems. They provide new challenges and opportunities for employees, warding off the kind of mental stagnation that leads to low morale, low quality, and low productivity. They also reduce employee turnover by eliminating dead-end jobs that force employees to look elsewhere for new challenges. And they offer incentives for employees to stay on their job when advancement and promotions are limited.

Perhaps most importantly, however, a pay-for-skills program allows employees to do what they do best. A top-flight physicist, for instance, can continue to do laboratory work and does not have to accept a management position just to earn more money; this scientist's income will increase as he or she acquires more technical knowledge. The company avoids losing an excellent researcher—and also avoids the expense of recruiting and training a replacement. At the same time, the company can fill its management positions with people who are better suited to be managers than scientists.

Companies that have adopted the pay-for-skills approach—like Procter & Gamble—have found that it also helps increase the business's flexibility. "We decided to pay people a weekly salary determined by the number of different jobs an individual can perform," explains Stanley Holditch, a former P&G manager. "There would be no time clocks or watchmen."

Under P&G's system, employees are divided into work groups, and as group members learn each other's jobs, their rates of pay are increased. Once an employee learns all the functions performed in a group, he or she then goes on to learn the functions of another group. Through cross-training, each employee masters more than just one skill and that means that workers can cover for one another in case of illness, or fill in when a key employee leaves the company. It also smoothes the apprenticeship of new employees, since everyone is knowledgeable enough to assist in the training. In addition, pay-for-skills programs give workers greater job security, because they can easily be moved to another position (which they have already been trained for) if their job happens to become obsolete.

For the police department in Palatine, Illinois, the adoption of a pay-for-skills program called the Dual Career Ladder (DCL) provided the solution to a low morale problem caused by too few promotion opportunities. Before DCL, officers had to wait for the death or retirement of a superior before they could advance, but DCL solved the problem by redesigning the traditional career ladder. Police personnel are now able to earn more money and receive greater recognition just by acquiring new skills within their area—fingerprinting, witness interrogation, or marksmanship, for example. Pay increases are authorized for a year. And to keep earning the increase, an officer must be recertified or must redemonstrate competence in these additional skills.

Palatine's Deputy Chief of Police, Walter Gasior, is enthusiastic about the multiple benefits of the program. "It improves their capabilities as professionals, enhances their performance as police officers, and maximizes overall performance of the department," he says. "What's more, it provides cost-effective police service to the community."

By developing the full potential of its police officers—and paying them more for it—Palatine has not only seen substantial improvements in morale, but has registered significant productivity gains as well. Since DCL was installed, in fact, Palatine has been able to reduce the total number of police personnel it employs, while at the same time increasing overall departmental productivity by 10 percent. "It's an effective management strategy," explains Gasior, "designed so that if we can meet the needs of our people, they will meet our needs, and we'll all be working toward the same goal."

Though it may be a lot simpler to hand out automatic, across-the-board raises based on seniority than to install a pay-for-skills program, companies that always take the easy road may actually be reducing the incentive for their people to develop new talents. Instead of getting more "bang" for their bucks, these organizations may be settling for just a flat fizzle.

JOB SECURITY

Money talks, as we have seen, but many nonmonetary rewards are also effective in motivating workers toward increased productivity. According to Carla O'Dell, a management consultant in employee motivation, "Many of the issues that set the stage for effective and rewarding organizations are not the ones you'd typically think of when you think of reward systems." Some of these nontraditional motivators include employee security, greater recognition and responsibility, and participative decision making.

A survey of 5,000 people employed in the private sector by the Wyatt Company revealed that overall job satisfaction was high—70 percent responding favorably—with 53 percent of the respondents satisfied with their salaries and 61 percent responding favorably about benefits overall. When asked about their satisfaction with overall management of their companies and how they were treated by management above their immediate superiors, less that 40 percent gave favorable ratings and 26 percent responded unfavorably. This confirms the richness of opportunities to improve employee interest, satisfaction and overall performance by addressing nontraditional areas for rewarding employees.

EMPLOYMENT SECURITY

Part of the general concern of workers about the overall performance of their companies has to do with their perceptions about the long-term job security provided by their employer.

More and more companies are finding that job security is a primary concern among their employees. In many instances, it has replaced pay and benefits as the principal bargaining issue between companies and labor unions. Yet competition makes it one of the most difficult guarantees for employers to provide. Recurring economic recessions and the growing menace of foreign competition mean that companies must be cost-effective competitors to survive and to maintain their position in the marketplace. But as markets and sales shrink, or as consumer buying patterns change, managers must utilize every means to keep themselves ahead. And sometimes the decline in sales is serious enough that people must be laid off.

Owners and managers put a high premium on keeping their company going, and employees, of course, put a high premium on job security. They want to know that they will be able to continue to work as long as they put in a good performance. The only way to satisfy all parties concerned, however, is to find ways to ensure that workers become increasingly more productive.

Still, there is a pervasive notion that improved productivity will result in the elimination of jobs, or that a company must reduce its work force in order to become more competitive. To many employees, productivity improvement becomes a "catch 22." By helping their company become more productive, they believe they are sowing the seeds of their own destruction. After all, they have seen workers in other companies build the gallows for their own hangings.

In truth, however, the productivity in those other firms probably went something like this: Due to increased competition, sales and sales revenues dropped. Management asked for help in reducing costs, and finally ended up laying off some employees in nonproductive jobs. When productivity initiatives were introduced, otherwise rational employees interpreted them as an effort to eliminate the need for their own jobs. They reacted by exaggerating the importance of every aspect of their work and consuming even more time in performing it. That made profits deteriorate even further, and managers had to look for additional ways to save money, such as letting more people go.

To avoid this downward spiral, however, one message to employees must be made perfectly clear: the company is committed to doing all it can to maintain the jobs of people who do good work. Only when employees are convinced that their company is committed to their continued employment will managers have the freedom to ask for cost savings and employees will feel secure enough to show managers how to achieve them.

Fordham University business professor Marta Mooney has found in her work with many companies that, among all workers, employment security is probably of greatest concern to middle managers. They have the most difficulty locating new jobs if laid off, and they are first to go when management layers have to be sacrificed. Yet, middle managers are the key to any productivity initiative, whether it starts at the top or bottom of a company. And in a company that does not consider employment security a priority, they are likely to become part of the productivity problem rather than part of the solution.

A number of major U.S. companies have developed strategies aimed at maximizing job security; IBM is one. "Some say full employment is a luxury only a company like ours can afford," says a senior IBM personnel officer. "Maybe we can afford it because we make the commitment, and because our people respond to that commitment with a business performance that makes it affordable. Concern for full employment—indeed job security—is the very foundation of increased productivity."

James Bolt, a former manager of human resources and development planning at Xerox who is now a university professor, points out that layoffs can be expensive, disruptive, and sometimes self-defeating. Layoffs mean the loss of training and experience the company has paid for over time. Some of the experience will not be available when the company starts to grow again. In addition, severance payments and recruitment are major costs for many companies. There are always many hidden costs involved in laying workers off, says Bolt. And once the process gets under way, the stress it imposes on the entire work force often results in the voluntary departure of many top-quality employees—regardless of whether or not their jobs are in jeopardy.

Recent business history shows that when labor and management work together, however, they can usually find ways of creating a workplace environment in which job security has priority. The Ford Motor Company and the United Auto Workers provide one example. They have set up a program jointly administered by the company and the union, to help retrain workers whose jobs have become endangered. Established under a Collective Bargaining Agreement, the UAW-Ford Employee Development and Training Program (EDTP) is funded by a Ford contribution of five cents per worker hour.

The EDTP encompasses four key areas: educational training and assistance; national vocational retraining assistance; targeted vocational retraining; and career counseling and guidance. At present, over 1,300 active Ford employees participate in the Education and Training Assistance Plan, which provides money for tuition at approved educational institutions, and 4,500 furloughed employees are taking advantage of the National Vocational Retraining Assistance Plan, which pays for courses related to the automotive and other industries. The Targeted Vocational Retraining Project helps over 650 laid-off employees receive technical training in occupations with immediate job opportunities, while over 2,000 furloughed employees have graduated from the Career Counseling and Guidance Program.

Naturally, very few companies are able to make a commitment of total job security to their employees, and those that do may find it impossible to carry out in the event of disastrous economic circumstances. Nevertheless, employment security should become a corporate objective that is integrated into business and financial planning, even though honoring this commitment may sometimes require creative and difficult management decisions. For companies that have successfully met the challenge, the benefits are obvious: employees are happier, morale is higher, and the company, on the whole, is more productive. As one IBM executive explains: "By using their minds as well as their hands, our people have cut two-thirds of the hours that go into manufacturing our product. The cost of the product went down 45 percent during a ten-year period when wages vastly increased. That achievement would have been impossible without productive and committed employees. And much of their commitment stems from the security they know is theirs."

How do you develop a job security program? Here are a few guidelines from companies that have successfully taken the plunge:

1. Adopt a formal corporate policy that demonstrates a commitment to employment security. Lincoln Electric, for example, guarantees all permanent, full-time employees a minimum of thirty hours of work a week for forty-nine weeks a year. Lincoln has always honored its commitment, even during the 1981–82 recession.

2. Develop recruitment and training programs that provide full employment for existing employees.

a) Hire and promote from within the company as much as possible. At Digital Equipment Corporation, a manufacturer of computer equipment, all hiring from outside the company must be approved by a senior vice-president.

b) Train and retrain employees in new skills to increase their job mobility *within* the firm. Procter & Gamble, for instance, provides incentives for employees to learn new skills so that they can cover for fellow workers during vacations, periods of illness, or emergencies. Besides keeping everyone fully employed, this policy also helps the company save on the cost of hiring temporary or free-lance workers.

c) Maintain a lean permanent work force that can be augmented, as needed, with planned overtime or temporary workers. At IBM, overtime, contract suppliers, and temporary personnel are used during periods of peak production. As one personnel administrator explains: "A buffer strategy is an important part of the planning process, because it means that if the work load falls short of expectations, for any reason, we can decrease overtime, reduce temporary assignments, or limit the work we vend to ensure full-time work for all our regular employees."

3. Guarantee continuity of employment by obtaining a commitment from employees or their union representatives for increased flexibility in job assignments, training, and relocation. When McCreary Tire and Rubber Company in Indiana, Pennsylvania, fell victim to a recession, management worked with employees to establish a work-furlough program. As an alternative to laying off a third of the work force, McCreary allowed each employee to work two weeks out of three during the summer, while it investigated additional cost-cutting measures and switched production from low-demand passenger car tires to high-margin truck and specialty tires. The State of Pennsylvania also agreed to pay supplemental unemployment benefits for the weeks employees were on furlough.

As a result, the company's payroll costs were reduced significantly, while productivity rose, absenteeism fell, and on-the-job injuries decreased. McCreary not only weathered the recession but emerged a lot stronger for it. "The payroll savings helped us through a tough time, and kept everyone on the job," a personnel supervisor observes. "We've been notorious in the last few years for losing money, but now we're a profitable firm."

During a subsequent labor strike, the furlough program was suspended. On March 3, 1988 employees voted against keeping the union, but management and employees are prepared to resurrect the program when their business encounters the next recession.

RECOGNITION

All too often, the only time workers hear from management is when their boss is displeased. With some justification, employees frequently complain that the only feedback they get is negative.

But all employees need to hear praise, too. And recognition for a job well done can help stimulate the desire to raise productivity and competitiveness. Well-fed egos can yield higher profits. Unfortunately, however, management usually ignores the large percentage of the labor force that does a good job and concentrates on the bottom five percent that does *not*.

A recognition program can result in amazing productivity dividends. And it need not be elaborate or expensive: an employee-of-the-month contest, free lunch on the company, a special company jacket, or just a chance to hear praise from the boss in front of co-workers or family members.

When Dan Boyle took over as personnel manager at Diamond International, he realized that nothing was being done for the majority of employees who did their job well. His perception was confirmed by a companywide survey showing that 65 percent of the employees felt they were not being treated respectfully, and 79 percent felt they were not being sufficiently rewarded. Low morale was reflected in the high number of monthly grievances—150—and the rate of absenteeism.

Under Boyle's direction, Diamond International introduced the "100 Club" at its egg carton plant in Palmer, Massachusetts, as a vehicle for recognizing employee contributions to the company. Employees were awarded points for performing certain aspects of their job well (25 points for perfect attendance, for example), and any employee who earned 100 points was inducted into the 100 Club, receiving a blue nylon jacket with a club patch. Additional points entitled members to free gifts. These gifts were not particularly extravagant (they were within a worker's purchasing power), but they served the purpose of the program: to demonstrate management's interest in and appreciation for good work.

Diamond International's workers heard the message loud and clear. With the program now installed in three additional plants, there has been a definite improvement in overall morale. According to a recent survey, in fact, 77 percent of the company's workers feel they are now being amply rewarded through recognition. Absenteeism has decreased by over 40 percent (resulting in savings of $114,462 in one year), and an independent analysis attributed savings of over $5 million to the Club program in an eighteen-month period—not a bad return for a total investment of only $100,000. For the past 5 years the 100 Club program has continued to generate an extra 2.3% growth per year in productivity for Diamond. In addition, Boyle has been hired to install it in another 60 plants for companies such as Owens Corning Fiberglass and Nestle Foods Corp. By the way, Boyle and a partner subsequently bought and renamed the Thorndike, Mass. plant Diamond Fiber Products.

JOB SATISFACTION AND ENRICHMENT

Many experts believe that the greatest reward any worker can receive is job satisfaction. We all tend to be more productive when we feel good about our job and our work surroundings. Keeping employees satisfied means constantly providing them with new challenges and new and different responsibilities. And one challenge that workers always seem eager to meet is participatory decision making. "The art of creating participation is a reward in itself," notes Irving DeToro of Xerox. "It allows for achievement, learning, and mastery over one's environment. And these rewards, in turn, can serve as powerful motivators for the achievement of organizational goals."

Ron Contino, deputy commissioner for support operations for New York City's Department of Sanitation, is one official who still gets excited when he talks about the reward potential of participation. "The process of getting labor involved in the running of an operation is not only exciting and rewarding," says Contino, it's also extremely worthwhile in terms of improving productivity and service quality."

When Contino took over departmental operations in 1978, the Bureau of Motor Equipment was widely recognized as being in a state of chaos. Almost half its sanitation trucks were inoperative on any given day, the amount of overtime was extraordinarily high and expensive, and substantial "rework" was constantly required.

To turn the bureau around, Contino gave employees greater control over their work environment by allowing them to participate in development, management, procurement, and budget programs. Repair and collection crews became involved in the evaluation of new equipment and worked with supervisors in establishing the specifications for collection vehicles. As a result, the equipment design manufacture of repair parts in-house has reduced purchasing costs while still maintaining parts inventory levels. Today, the bureau's repair shops are operating at a "profit center" productivity level. In fact, every dollar the city invests in its operation has been calculated to be worth $1.41 in goods and services purchased from the private sector.

Increasing job responsibility is another way that employers can show their appreciation for the way workers do their job. Being presented with new challenges is intrinsically rewarding to employees, and it enables managers to redeploy their own time more productively. For example, allowing a good secretary to screen calls and clients, write original letters, and handle routine executive matters frees up the boss for more demanding matters and reinforces the recognition of the secretary's capabilities.

Fab Steel, which fabricates petrochemical plant steel superstructures, is one company that has successfully expanded employee responsibility with its individual Triangle of Responsibility Program for managers. The "Triangle" concept brings managers to focus in three ways: on their own principal tasks, on overall company competitiveness, and on helping one another in different parts of the company. Champion International is another. It encourages increased responsibility and better management through the Managing for Excellence Program, which trains "high potential" managers in finance and human resource development.

FINDING THE PERFECT MIX

Some companies find that a single program of rewards provides adequate incentives, but usually it takes a mix of techniques—profit sharing, recognition systems, bonuses, job satisfaction—to create a truly productive and competitive environment. You might find a cash bonus system to be good for rewarding your employees who come up with ideas for resolving bottlenecks, for instance, but an ESOP may be your best way to motivate them toward increased sales.

Whatever reward system you design, however, you should make sure that it works to achieve your company's objectives—as does Amway's. A direct sales company, Amway has developed a sophisticated reward and recognition system to motivate its independent distributors, who number more than a million. Distributors earn commissions based on the retail product sales they make. But they also receive commissions—and performance bonuses—based on the income generated by the new salespeople they sponsor. Since a sponsoring distributor is responsible for paying his or her team members their performance bonus when they in turn sponsor others, the fortunes of distributors and sponsors are inextricably linked. Employees are rewarded for their individual efforts as well as for those of their group, and a distributor succeeds, in effect, through the success of those he or she sponsors. But nothing is paid unless a sale is made, because at Amway, sale is the name of the game.

Amway distributors are also recognized in other important ways: as sales volume increases, they become eligible for awards and designations—pins, plaques, trips, and cars. And anytime anyone achieves a new sales plateau, a profile of that person is featured in *Amagram*, the company magazine.

Amway uses its reward system to help it succeed in constantly changing market conditions. At the present time, the company is focusing on greater sales per distributor rather than on the recruitment of new salespeople. Productivity and competitiveness means building on their existing strength in existing salespeople. As other companies copy their direct sales methods, the skills of the experienced sales representatives are what makes Amway more competitive. They have no special advantage if Amway is only hiring the same type of new people that their competitors are seeking. So the plan now provides additional bonuses for gains in sales by individual distributors. These new incentives seem to be producing the desired result: Amway sales—which totaled $500,000 in 1959—have grown to almost $2 billion today.

Rewarding employees should be seen not as a way of buying allegiance, but as a way of demonstrating management interest and concern in the people who are an essential part of the organization. After all, when you are facing competition on a global scale, it pays to have team members who are committed to a common cause, rather than mercenaries who are committed only to themselves.

Any manufacturing operation that is not actively pursuing new capital investment—productivity improving investment—is a factory on death row.

—Jules Mirabel, Technology Manager, General Electric Company

9

INVESTMENT: Capitalizing New Technology and Research

Investing in research and technology is one of the great hallmarks of American business. In the past, our inventions and innovations propelled American industry to the number one position among world competitors. But as our ability and inclination to remain the leader declined, so has our competitive position.

It was once said that "the U.S. can outinvent the rest of the world combined." So far, we still do. However, U.S. companies are beginning to falter in their ability to *continue* to apply inventiveness to their products, services, and marketing. For example, the VCR—commercial and retail video recording technology— is an American invention. But when American companies decided not to pursue the market opportunity, the Japanese developed it. The challenge to many American businesses now, therefore, is to regain control of their great American inventiveness and technology to create the right products.

Keeping up-to-date on new manufacturing or service techniques is a primary responsibility of management. And making sure that new investments in offices and plants embody the right technology equipment is an important second step. And finally, employees need to know how to use their new tools effectively.

FROM STONES TO COMPUTERS

Determining how humans and technology work together most effectively is not a new challenge. From the very beginning, man has designed, built, and bought

58

tools to make work easier. Crudely shaped cutting and digging instruments were as crucial to ancient survival as computers and assembly lines are to the economics of the 1980s. Long before the concept of capital investment was recognized, all laborers knew that tasks could be accomplished a lot more easily with tools.

So man learned early on to invest in the future. "Don't eat your seed corn or use your fence posts for firewood" is an old saying that embodies this lesson. Even back then, capital investment in tools, education, and research always meant "less now for more later." But today, as the speed of change accelerates, investment requirements are increasing exponentially.

AUTOMATION IS MORE THAN WORKING FASTER

Automation has been a buzzword for several decades now. Though it often conjures up negative images—little Charlie Chaplins working faster and faster until they spin into a frenzy—it also means having machines to do the work of people. And that can result in increased sales, easier jobs, better working conditions, and more business opportunities.

The accelerated growth of technology—most recently by combining microprocessing capabilities with electrical and electronic equipment—has multiplied both the problems and the opportunities of investing today. Computers can collect, analyze, and relay information between people and machines, improving productivity and competitiveness through the better management of information, production, services, and sales. But even the most sophisticated computer system is useless without trained operators: it is people that make technology work. A computerized accounting operation can be worse than a pen and ledger if it is operated improperly.

Some managers also fail to realize that increased investment in equipment and technology does not automatically result in higher productivity. Too much of a good thing can be bad for you. If you increase your capital investment levels too quickly and without proper planning, trouble lies ahead. Up to a point, your investments may provide increased returns, but the more you spend, the worse off you could be.

IT WON'T BITE YOU

Payoffs through technology require a certain level of awareness by all managers and employees, whether in manufacturing or service industries. And overcoming fear of technology is an initial step in developing this awareness. Most people fear what they do not understand. They quickly reject what is new and create mental blocks against that which they feel uninformed about. As a manager, you do not have to get to the root of these psychological fears. But you do need to recognize that they exist and develop programs to make technology better understood and less threatening for your people.

General Electric, for example, conquers "technophobia" by setting up new robotics equipment in employee lunchrooms. In this unthreatening environment, workers can see, touch, and play with new equipment and learn how it works. Without pressure, they can discover why it is to their advantage to adopt a new way.

Some workers also fear automation because they think it will make their job obsolete. They resist the introduction of machines, robots, or computers rather than welcoming them as tools that will enhance their work and protect them from the ravages of foreign competition. When this happens, it is management's responsibility to show workers how technology can actually save their job by making their company more competitive.

General Electric faced this challenge when it decided to automate its 70-year-old locomotive plant in Erie, Pennsylvania, with new computer-controlled machine tools and computer-aided design, engineering, and manufacturing systems. Automation did reduce the number of workers required to produce each locomotive, but the total number of jobs in Erie actually increased because the lower prices that resulted from automation increased the demand for the GE trains.

Glen Watts, retired president of the Communication Workers of America, once opposed technology—until he saw what it could do for his union members. He even resisted the introduction of dial telephones at first, because he thought they would put operators out of work. But the new technology made telephoning so inexpensive that, within a few years, the volume of calls dramatically outstripped the available pool of operators. In fact, if all calls were still operator-assisted today, the services would far exceed the industry's ability to provide them—even if every person in America were to become an operator!

TOTAL TECHNOLOGICAL AWARENESS

Eliminating technophobia may be an important first step in creating the kind of environment in which innovation can flourish; but it alone is not enough to create a positive technological climate. To do that, technology must be understood at all levels of the organization, and everyone must be looking for ways to apply it.

TRW, a multi-billion-dollar industrial electronics manufacturer, learned the value of "seeding" technological awareness at every level when it had to wrestle with problems in its own internal communications network. Because the company had worked hard to foster technological awareness, it turned to its own people to help solve the problems it was facing.

The company started by convening an internal management problem-solving group, one of whose members suggested an electronic mail and message system. Then another task force determined exactly what the company's needs were and, after analyzing its own efficiencies and costs, decided to hire an outside firm that specialized in system installation, rather than research and design, which is TRW's forte.

The chosen technology—a word processing and electronic mail system that instantly interfaces all parts of the company—has effectively closed the intra-company communications gap. Each division within TRW can now maintain its own electronic bulletin board, standardize communications lists for simultaneous delivery to managers throughout the world, edit and forward new messages, and reroute incoming messages.

The biggest benefits, however, have come from eliminating the need for workers to play long-distance telephone tag. Differing time zones are no longer a problem because messages can now be sent anywhere at anytime—whether or not the intended recipient is at work. And with portable computers, even traveling employees can send and receive messages.

As a result, the time it takes TRW managers to make decisions has been slashed by 50 percent. Company telephone costs have also been cut 15 percent, and overall communications productivity has improved substantially.

RUNNING FASTER JUST TO KEEP UP

Another reason for keeping employees technologically aware: they help ensure what you sell does not become outdated in the marketplace. When competitors start introducing more advanced models than you produce, you have to move faster than the competition just to keep pace. The accelerated rate of technological change today challenges even high-technology leaders. The makers of integrated circuit boards, for example, introduce new chips almost annually, and sales and market shares are won by those who offer the most powerful and the least expensive. In such a ruthless competitive environment, today's winner can easily become tomorrow's loser.

Honeywell was one firm that had to struggle with the issue of high-tech obsolescence. Although it was a major producer of integrated office and computer systems, it had failed to direct its technological antenna inward: Honeywell's own field operations were burdened with an inefficient system for internal communications. The company found itself in the curious position of having to use systems for word processing, data communications, the remote entry of sales and accounting information, and the transmission of information to regional networks that were not as up-to-date or efficient as those it provided to its own customers.

An internal service organization was commissioned by senior management to survey the company's needs, and in the end, it recommended the development and installation of the Office Administrative Support and Information System (OASIS), which now provides Honeywell with integrated communications services. By using OASIS, Honeywell expects a return of 20 percent each year on its initial $5-million investment. And as an added benefit, the company has a new and well-tested system it can now market to its customers.

Companies like Bell Atlantic, Softool, and Federal Express are also working to make sure they will not be caught off guard by new technology. By constantly investing in research and development, and by using a capital investment strategy consistent with the current market, they are staying ahead of the technology curve, and reaping healthy profits as well.

By developing cellular phone technology, Bell Atlantic thought it could apply an old concept to a new market: those who spend time working in their cars or at remote job sites. Realizing that this new market could contribute significantly to its future growth, the company made investment in this area a high priority. Advertising efforts were geared to showing businesses how cellular telephones could make employees more productive. When customers were ready to buy, Bell Atlantic had the new product already on the shelves.

Softool decided to capitalize on the irony of the automators being unautomated. It uses computer and special software to aid in the development and management of computer software systems. Controlling new versions and revisions of software, data, graphics and ordinary text will be less monumental with the aid of the computer used to generate them. Softool has targeted that opportunity.

From the beginning, Federal Express saw that the value in the service it provided was the quick transmission of information—not just paper and packages—from one point to another. The overnight mail system it developed in 1973 depended in part, on the computerized control of information, which has assured almost 100 percent reliability in delivery. A forward-thinking concept, made affordable through technology, became an overwhelming success for Federal Express.

But the company's ZAP mail service—which could transmit information between offices within hours using high-speed telefax machines—fizzled after an uninspiring launch. It was an example of how technology can be used to offer a service that was not worth the effort and expense to its potential customers. Federal Express failed to realize that companies with a need to transmit written communications quickly would rather invest in telefax equipment themselves, since the cost of the technology had decreased so significantly. Even companies that aggressively try to anticipate and cultivate the needs of their customers sometimes fail.

No matter how good your technology, you do not have a business unless you have customers who are eager to buy the product or service you sell. Here are six suggestions to keep in mind when trying to develop an investment-based technology awareness in your company:

1. Make developing and adopting new ways of doing things an explicit company objective. Talk about it at management meetings, and make it a part of each manager's job. Make sure that everyone keeps abreast of what is happening in the industry—or at least what the competition is doing. If you emphasize this approach consistently, it is sure to become a part of your corporate culture, and employees will continually work at finding improvements.

2. Let all employees know what new ideas are under development by the

company, its suppliers, customers, and competitors. You may not need state-of-the-art equipment, but you should be aware of what is available, especially if your competitor knows about it. It is always better to consider and rule out an option, than to have missed an opportunity that someone else might pursue.

3. Hold employees responsible for keeping up-to-date on technological developments in their area. Emphasize the benefits of technology and productivity to their job performance, job security, and pay. Make sure they understand—and you need to do more than just tell them—that technology is a tool *for* them and a weapon *against* the competition.

4. Provide technical journals, trade magazines, and other materials for employees. Encourage them to take these materials home and clip items for the company bulletin board or newsletters. Most employees are more interested in doing this than you might think; they often delight in explaining new methods and machines to their family, friends, and colleagues.

5. Train and educate all employees in the use of computers. Once an intimidated employee has had even rudimentary hands-on experience—as simple as typing a command and getting a response—fears and inhibitions will quickly begin to dissipate. Put an extra terminal, loaded with useful software, in the employee lunch area lounge. Almost no job in America is untouched by computers. Knowing how they work makes living with them a lot easier, and familiarity helps employees think about how they can be used to make the company more productive, more profitable, and more competitive.

6. Find out about government programs that assist companies in identifying available and useful technology. The Pennsylvania Technical Assistance Program, for example, helps direct companies toward the kind of technological information that will help them stay competitive. The Federal Laboratory Consortium also disseminates information to help businesses develop new products and processes.

SAVING TIME AND MONEY WITH TECHNOLOGY

The true value of technological awareness is only apparent, however, when you develop a new technology that allows you to meet and beat the competition. Surviving world-class competition these days usually requires a working knowledge of how to use technology to your best advantage.

When boatloads of inexpensive and high quality foreign products began landing on U.S. shores in the 1970s, Americans awoke to a new reality. The U.S. steel industry found that it could not compete with imports that relied on newer methods of production and cheaper labor—and that its management methods were equally obsolete. Rigid patterns of conformity were depriving the industry of new and better ideas and innovations.

And steel was not alone. U.S. automakers, the consumer electronics industry, textile manufacturers, and a sizeable portion of the industrial sector faced a similar rude awakening. Foreign imports were not basically different from their American counterparts, but they were a better buy—and we all know, Americans love to buy bargains.

General Electric is one corporation that changed to meet the foreign challenge. Facing stiff and growing competition, the company realized it had only three choices: automate, emigrate (move production offshore to take advantage of cheaper labor and materials), or evaporate.

In GE's dishwasher division, for example, foreign-made machines were infiltrating an already highly competitive domestic market. But the real problem GE identified was its own: its high-volume production system was obsolete, and competitors were able to underprice it by relying on innovative just-in-time production methods. Instead of warehousing large and costly inventories, as did GE, they used computers to schedule parts and supply deliveries to arrive ''just in time'' for last-minute assembly.

Refusing to get out of the business—evaporate—or even settle for a number two position, GE began to invest in high-tech automation and production redesign. The company developed a just-in-time, point-of-use manufacturing system, in which computer-controlled machines assemble parts on a as-needed basis at a location close to the main assembly line.

In assembling the tub units for GE dishwashers, for example, four punch presses each make a different part of the tub. The dishwasher control panels are produced at an adjacent location, and when complete, are automatically placed on a conveyor belt and moved about fifty feet to where computer-controlled machines attach them to the tub units. Robots then place the completed tub on an overhead conveyor, and in this manner, a tub is completed every ten seconds. Quality control—assuring that the product is ''bug free''—is handled by yet another computer, which will not allow production to continue if a unit is not properly assembled. The system is also flexible enough to accommodate product modifications, so that GE can adapt to changing consumer tasks on demand.

For GE, a bold investment in new technology has paid off handsomely. The new system substantially reduced inventory and production expenses at the dishwasher plant, cutting labor, materials, and overhead costs 10 percent and raising overall productivity 25 percent, while improving product quality as well. In fact, eighteen months after instituting the new system, consumer warranty complaints on GE dishwashers had declined by 53 percent. Most importantly, however, GE has been able to retain its customers, its position in the market place, and a profitable product line.

Here are six strategies that successful companies like GE have found effective in making technology work for them:

1. Make sure that company objectives go beyond just technological awareness. Look for obstacles that have crept into your policy and operating manuals, and change those things that you think may impede technology. Even high-tech companies find that their corporate procedures can stand in the way of automa-

tion. At one well-known firm, for example, employees were being paid less for operating a new machine than they were for handcrafting the product.

2. Reevaluate your proposed capital acquisitions against what the marketplace has to offer that is new. Buy what you have always purchased only if nothing else is available.

3. Design your service or product line and your production operations to maximize the use of technology. And do not force a new technology into an old way of doing things.

4. Automate in stages if you cannot automate an entire process. Let your suppliers know what your overall automation goals are so that they can advise you of equipment purchases that will contribute to your long-term objectives.

5. Integrate people and machines. That means involving employees from the beginning, and making sure that technology helps—not hinders—their work. Always provide adequate training so that employees will use and maintain their equipment properly.

6. Above all, plan for the long term. Work with local high schools and colleges; keep them apprised of the technical skills you are looking for and allow them to become familiar with your equipment. Tell them about the educational deficiencies that you think are impeding your productivity, and let them know just how important technology is to your success.

EVERYBODY IN THE POOL

Many small companies think that technology is just for the big guy. "We're too small to afford it" or "We don't have the capital to compete" are common complaints. But size should not be an obstacle. You can pool your resources with other organizations, if necessary, to take advantage of technological breakthroughs. By combining capital and talent, you can find the resources to solve industry problems or tackle projects that you alone could not undertake. Following are some examples of how cooperation has led to higher productivity and sales through technology.

Eight small businesses got together a few years ago to form the Small Business Technology Group, Inc., to bid on contracts to construct high-technology systems. Their first customer: the Air Force Electronics Systems Division and Development Center. Alone, none of the companies could have met the bidding requirements of the Air Force, nor did any one company have all the know-how to develop the desired electronics system. But collectively, sharing both risks and rewards, they succeeded. And by combining their marketing efforts, they now aggressively seek out new clients for their technological talents.

Jack Rennie, a founder of the Small Business Technology Group, approaches big production opportunities boldly. "A lot of times the government would rather grant a single multi-function contract. This has the effect of cutting out small businesses, because they can't qualify as the primes." But by pooling resources, he notes, little companies can still go after the big contracts, while subcontracting out the work involved that they are ill-equipped to handle.

The strategy of pooling resources together is not limited to small companies, however. Rather than lamenting the government support for computer development in Japan, William Norris, chairman of Control Data Corporation, decided to fight back. He recruited six other major computer companies to form Microelectronics Computer Corporation (MCC). Its goal: to tackle the development of next-generation computers. With the combined resources of its member companies, MCC can afford to fund the kind of basic research that will help assure U.S. supremacy in the supercomputer race. Its participants believe that MCC will give them the choice to remain competitive in the world market, even though the value of their cooperative efforts will not be known for many years.

Forming a Research and Development Limited Partnership (RDLP) is another way resources and knowledge can be combined to tackle innovations or inventions that are too much for one company to handle. An RDLP pools the financial and sometimes technical resources of several investors or participants to support an R&D effort, and each participant's liability is limited to its initial investment. If the effort succeeds and a new technology, production process, or product results, the investors receive a payback from its sale or licensing. In addition, an investing partner may have a special right to license the technology for use in its own company; this enables it to acquire a technology made possible through a joint effort. The partnership may also be structured in such a way that one company obtains exclusive use of the technology and pays the others for its use.

Genentech Inc., an innovator in genetic engineering, used this approach when it was faced with a pressing need to raise capital. The company considered licensing its new human growth hormone ("HGH") and gamma interferon technology to a foreign country, but instead it decided to raise $55 million through an RDLP and share the profits from its HGH technology with some outside investors. In this way, Genentech was able to retain control over its new product, preserve its equity ownership, and still raise enough money to see its innovation through to FDA approval.

Cooperation has never been customary in the garment industry, which historically has been composed of competitive, independent companies. Highly labor intensive, it is also an industry that has traditionally designed and used capital equipment for individual tasks such as folding, cutting, or sewing, and few attempts were made to upgrade this technology. But foreign competition forced manufacturers to choose between moving their plants overseas or taking strategic action.

Some clothing companies chose to fight back by forming the Tailored Clothing Technical Corporation. Using its joint funding, they were able to work with Draper Laboratory to develop new robotic sewing systems—technologies that no one company could have funded alone. Now in place, these systems are helping to reduce manufacturing costs for men's apparel throughout the country. And the companies and unions that make up the corporation are confident that they may finally have found a way to give America's hard-hit garment industry a crucial edge.

COMPUTERS IN THE WORKPLACE

So far, we have concentrated on the "how to" of developing technology awareness, and on the different strategies for integrating technology into a business. Now we will describe some of the ways computers are working to make companies more competitive. We will see how they are controlling assembly lines, mass producing complex parts, customizing products, managing inventories, and even helping to make better sales calls.

A Distributed Computer Control (DCC) system, for example, is a group of microprocessors that can be used to direct all the different functions in a manufacturing process. A network connects these microprocessors to each other and then to a large macro- or minicomputer, which monitors, supervises, and controls the entire system. Simply by monitoring the supervisory computer, an operator can oversee production and pinpoint problems within a whole plant. And because each microprocessor operates independently, a problem in one area does not have to affect any other part of the system.

DCCs eliminate the need to spend time setting switches and turning knobs. An operator no longer has to run down to the plant floor to see how things are going; it can be done from a central location. As one technology manager at Squibb describes it: "We've taken everything that an operator would do if he were sitting twenty-four hours a day and programmed it into our Distributed Computer Control system."

A plant with a DCC system has several advantages over a plant where everything is controlled by a single computer. In a single-system plant, growth can be cumbersome, costly, and slow, and single systems are frequently unable to implement several complex manufacturing strategies simultaneously. Though a single computer can be connected to all parts of a plant at the same time, it cannot retrieve and process all the information at once. This can slow down production, idling operating machines and conveyors while they wait for the master computer to shift and sort information, and then respond with further instructions.

General Motors improved its DCC operations by making all its computer-controlled systems capable of communicating with each other, regardless of how many different types of systems the company bought. As an example of how its factories of the future will work, GM demonstrated how workstations designed by twenty-five different computer equipment manufacturers could be interconnected so that machines, computers, and people can all communicate directly. By establishing common software protocols, GM plans to extend the system to suppliers and retail sales networks as well.

Although the initial cost of setting up a DCC system can be substantial, many companies with them report that the productivity gains they make help pay off the system in a relatively short period of time. Exxon Chemical Company, for example, spent $500,000 installing a DCC system that controls temperatures, pressures, and raw materials flow in its chemical reactors, but the company expects to recoup its initial investment in only two years.

Computer Numerically Controlled (CNC) systems are another technological breakthrough that help manufacturers to mass produce complex parts and products. In a CNC system, detailed instructions for performing a particular task, such as boring, shaping, cutting, or drilling, are fed into a computer that operates a specific machine. And since program controls do not vary from piece to piece, companies that use CNC systems in their assembly lines find that scrap, waste, and rework are eliminated because their machines can now make the product right each and every time.

Huron Machine Products found that the initial cost of its CNC equipment could be easily recovered because, once programmed, its machines do not have to be set, tested, and reset. In addition, one Huron employee can easily operate several machines simultaneously, because each machine can perform multiple tasks without being reset for each task by its operator. CNC systems also improve safety conditions since employees are no longer moving stock through moving blades and other cutting devices. Employees with lower skill levels and less training are able to perform tasks previously reserved for skilled workers, thereby lowering labor costs and increasing labor pool flexibility.

Before the introduction of computerized systems, certain production processes required careful control to assure uniform quality. Metal casting, for example, was as much an art as a science. But one manufacturer, Amcast Industrial Corporation of Dayton, Ohio, was able to eliminate the guesswork and make steel production a lot easier by using computer systems to monitor and record all the conditions necessary to producing good steel. By carefully controlling the production environment according to these specifications, Amcast is now able to duplicate the very best conditions continually and can produce a high-quality steel that is easily competitive with all foreign imports.

Deere & Company integrated its CNC equipment with a DCC system to produce a Flexible Manufacturing System (FMS) that can customize products for specific clients. Rather than having to batch production runs (i.e., fill all orders for a certain product at a single time), the company merely has to feed quantity, model, style, and size specifications into a computer and its manufacturing equipment automatically adjusts to specific orders as they are received.

Using an FMS, Deere & Company can customize each and every tractor it produces, and it accrues substantial money savings in many production areas. Inventories of finished goods are reduced because there is no need to store extra items to make batch runs feasible. Setup time for production equipment is practically eliminated, manufacturing is easier since the right parts are always introduced into the assembly process at just the right time.

Manufacturing large numbers of parts and maintaining huge inventories to support assembly operations can often result in mismatched production timetables. But by using computers to control production scheduling—as Boeing does in its jet aircraft plants—a manufacturer can easily resolve any parts delivery and assembly delay problems.

Parts unavailability and the incorrect sequencing of assembly line processes used to result in production delays at Boeing ranging from four hours to four days on a single plane. But now a computerized scheduling and inventory control system automatically chooses the optimal assembly sequence and assures that parts are available as needed. By eliminating overtime and overhead resulting from production delays, Boeing has improved both its productivity and profitability.

Similarly, General Electric found that installing a production scheduling system at its Wilmington, North Carolina, aircraft plant has increased productivity 30 percent there, while achieving a 30 to 40 percent reduction in inventory expenses. Efficiencies resulted because the system was able to work out a production timetable that achieves maximum machine utilization and streamlines parts and raw materials delivery schedules.

One of the easiest, yet most productive, uses of computers in manufacturing and service industries is improving inventory control. Humana Inc., a large for-profit health organization, found that a computerized inventory control system allows it to benefit from economies of scale by controlling purchasing for its 17,000-bed acute-care facilities. By monitoring supplies throughout the hospital system from a central computer at its Louisville headquarters, Humana estimates that it saved $85 million in three years.

Further efficiencies—and cost savings—can result when a company ties its inventory control system to its storage facilities. General Electric, for example, was considering abandoning its meter production plant in Somerset, New Hampshire, because it was simply running out of room there. But instead, the company built an addition on the roof and designed a materials handling system that make the multi-level facility as efficient as a single-floor plant. The new system utilizes two conveyor networks and three automated storage systems. GE used computers to integrate the storage and inventory systems at Somerset and converted the space above the production floor to a storage facility. The manufacturing system is now connected by conveyor networks to the 40,000-foot storage system overhead.

"The dog had learned new tricks," says Jules Mirabel, a GE technology manager. "We moved in computers, lasers, robots, and a highly advanced materials handling system. It's still an old-looking building from the outside, but inside those meters are pouring out."

Robots are another computer technology that is being used more frequently in production. They are especially good for jobs that are monotonous, offensive, or simply dangerous. Using robots for spray painting, for example, which involves exposure to toxic substances, can make the work place safer and even improve the quality of paint operations. Steelcase, the country's largest office furniture manufacturer, has found that robots use less paint, do a more uniform job, and are more productive. And the employees they replace can be retrained and reassigned to other positions.

THE HUMAN SIDE OF TECHNOLOGY

Automating information services is one of the most common and efficient ways to use computers. Sophisticated electronic typewriters, word processors, and personal computers can substantially reduce the amount of time spent processing information, analyzing large quantities of data, and keeping accounting records. But computers do more than just save time. At Memorial Hospital, for example, a 600-bed facility in Houston, Texas, it was found that doctors and nurses worked better when a centralized information processing system was installed to create, maintain, and process patient records.

Training, counseling, making medical diagnoses, and many other functions that rely on interactions between people can frequently be performed more reliably and at lower costs with computers. Automated education and training modules that permit an employee to proceed at his or her own pace are often more effective than classroom training geared to the "average" student. They are also more convenient (can be scheduled any time the employee is free), offer privacy and anonymity (encouraging the user to respond more frankly), and can be programmed to provide positive reinforcement. And when education is computerized, there is no danger of a personality clash between teacher and student.

Computerized counseling services enable managers to respond to unique personnel problems with solutions that incorporate the collective wisdom of a wide range of experts. Such systems also allow employees to deal with certain personal issues on their own. An employee can tell the computer about a particular problem he or she is having: difficulty in arriving to work on time, for example, or lack of motivation—and the computer will select a variety of approaches for solving it.

Computers have also been found to be effective at helping people to sell and market products by storing and retrieving market information, sales trends, customer profiles, credit information, and descriptions of product lines. J. C. Penney recognized early on the part computers could play in retailing. During the 1960s, it pressed suppliers to install point-of-sales terminals so that it could control inventory, identify customer buying patterns, and thus better respond to customer needs.

A competitor, Sears, Roebuck and Co., found that information stored in its computer system could help it "cross sell" services. As a new-product warranty nears expiration, for example, the Sears system generates a letter to the customer to recommend an extended warranty contract. And the purchase of the new service can be billed automatically to the client's account.

REMINDER

As a manager, none of your responsibilities is more important than knowing how to choose and use the right technology. With it, you can select products and services appropriate for your business, design and make them without error, and sell them more effectively. So invest the time and energy to understand and use this capital resource. It is an unending challenge, but one that can keep your company a successful and profitable competitor.

We have, by far, the most supportive conditions anywhere in the world: the most advanced technology, an incomparable industrial infrastructure, an incredible entrepreneurial culture, the best capital formation capability, the world's largest market, and a common language. We have everything in spades.
—D. Bruce Merrifield,
Commerce Department official and
former Fortune 500 executive

10

THE AMERICAN ADVANTAGE:
Regaining the Competitive Edge

America has extraordinary and abundant economic resources. It has created a technological base that is unsurpassed in size, a skilled labor force, unparalleled opportunities for education and training, and vast capital markets. It provides a competitive advantage that is there for the taking. The challenge now is to use these resources to regain our position as the preeminent, world-class competitor.

Among America's greatest assets is our free market, capitalist system, which allows the constant creation of new enterprises and new jobs. In 1985 and 1986, for example, over 600,000 new companies were formed in America each year, and from 1982 to 1987, about 15,000,000 new jobs were created.

Our economic freedom and the flexibility we have to move about, to change careers and employers, and to make our own luck surpasses that of any other country in the world. This freedom is more than a theoretical concept. It gives entrepreneurs and employees the right to choose where they work and, in greater measure than anywhere else, with whom they work. And it also gives employers a tremendously diverse pool of talent.

The freedom to associate and to form new enterprises is the essence of the entrepreneurial spirit in America; it is just easier to conceive and start a new business here than in other countries. Knowing that helps make Americans more creative by nature and stimulates a greater degree of entrepreneurial behavior.

New, smaller businesses are large contributors to productivity and job creation. They arise because their founders believed they could reap the rewards of becoming superior competitors. And existing businesses can take advantage of that initiative in many ways: by allowing new companies to grow within existing companies, by capitalizing entrepreneurs and promoting their ideas, and by developing new services and products for larger markets.

The freedom to compensate and reward at will (instead of according to mandated plans, as is common in many other countries) gives U.S. employers the right to choose those incentives they think will best motivate their people. Being able to provide job security programs without being compelled to do so by the government, for example, makes such programs seem like a reward to workers rather than an entitlement.

Profit sharing and stock ownership plans are also more attractive in the U.S. because of the opportunities here to start, build, and expand companies. The breadth of capital and securities markets makes employee ownership a more viable alternative. Traditionally a nation of owners rather than renters, we Americans are more receptive to ownership motivation. And because of our relatively classless society, we often can and do aspire beyond our current station because we know that social barriers can be easily overcome. When a work force is just waiting to meet the competition and is eager to win, managers need only to know how to open the starting gates.

Many books have been written about the benefits of a free, competitive society and its ability to create a productive environment. They cannot overstate the importance of economic freedom. It is part of the American heritage, and it can be a supremely valuable asset in becoming more productive, more competitive, and more profitable.

A CAPITAL IDEA

America's capital markets are the largest and, more importantly, the most efficient in the world. Money is available here to support creative ideas and innovative technology, which are the lifeblood of healthy competition. In the last five years, initial public stock offerings have raised $65 billion for their companies, and established firms have raised $87 billion by selling additional shares. That means that more than $152 billion in new funds have been available to promote new ideas, build new plants, buy new equipment, fund new product lines, and pay off debts—all of which are essential ingredients to becoming more competitive. And even more money awaits offshore, as foreign capital markets continue to supply our growth.

Some businesses have taken advantage of this capital in ways that have led them to higher levels of growth and profitability. But other businesses have had to learn the hard way that management's failure to use capital productively can result in losing the competitive edge. The many cases of companies that elected not to use their capital assets to modernize and grow are well known. A good example within the copper industry is Anaconda Copper, which has substantially left the business while Phelps Dodge has used its capital to develop a new process that cut the cost of producing copper by 50%. Anaconda went another route that led it to the evaporation point. Phelps Dodge has grown to become the largest and most competitive U.S. copper producer. Another example is Nucor Steel's use of continuous casting to outcompete much larger companies such as U.S. Steel. A long list of steel companies went out of business because they failed to spend their capital on the new technologies. But unfortunately, we know only anecdotally the names of those small ventures that made good use of capital markets to raise funds for productive enterprise.

One of the most important roles that government can play in making American companies more competitive is to provide an economic climate that promotes saving and investment. Removing disincentives to save and invest should always be high on the list of those seeking government action, but even more important is the assurance of a stable, low-inflation business environment. That alone is enough to bring U.S. and foreign capital out looking for new ideas to support.

STOREHOUSE OF KNOWLEDGE

The U.S. is unparalleled in the abundance of information it provides people about inventions, innovations, new technologies, and new techniques. Universities, government research laboratories, business enterprises, and productivity centers are all storehouses of knowledge on how to improve productivity and profits. And most of this information is freely available to anyone who wants to know about it. Unfortunately, many people think that what is free has little value.

Most government research centers are open to the public, and their scientists are usually eager to help companies in need. Many have also discovered brilliant solutions to nagging business problems—solutions that are only waiting to be picked up by a company willing to bring them to market. Still, the "not invented here" syndrome keeps most companies away from federal labs. Also, there are even greater opportunities awaiting those who will just take the time to look—and the variety is infinite, from flat-panel displays to devices that can measure the amount of lean meat in ground beef. Either technology could make a clever entrepreneur a handsome return by carving out a premier market niche.

America is truly the invention capital of the world. And over 90 percent of the new knowledge that becomes available each year comes from government- and industry-sponsored research, which government offices and educational institutions are only too willing to share. Many also provide clearinghouses to disseminate the kind of information about technology, productivity, and the characteristics of successful businesses that would be helpful to the competition-minded manager.

GOVERNMENT IN THE ECONOMY

In recent years, there has been much talk about the importance of fortifying the "supply side" of the American economy. That means, at least politically, the country has been advocating the goals of increased productivity and efficiency, sometimes without knowing it. Cutting taxes that go to pay for health care, education, and police and fire protection, while still maintaining or even augmenting existing services, can only be brought about through higher productivity. And saving the environment means using it more sparingly and efficiently.

All political parties appear to support actions that will promote growth, jobs, higher incomes, and a more competitive economy. Some talk about freezing out the competition through tariffs or other trade barriers, but that strategy can be successful only in the short term and will be counterproductive down the line. The only real solution, of course, is to become more productive and competitive in the private sector.

There is a lot of talk these days about unfair competition and unlevel playing fields. There is no doubt about it: competition is not always fair, and sometimes can be pretty rough. So when you are trying to compete, you had better be willing to use all the resources at your disposal: people, technology, the commitment to quality, and basic American ingenuity. Fighting to win means using everything you've got.

LAND OF INFINITE VARIETY

In this world economy where we must all now compete, the diversity of the American people may turn out to be one of our greatest natural assets. Because of it, all the different talents of the world—every race, creed, nationality, religion, and culture—are available within our borders. Employers can draw from this diverse pool of backgrounds and talents in selecting their work forces and finding the special experts that will help them become sharp shooters.

Some will cite the Far East as an example in arguing that ethnic uniformity always gives a country a competitive edge. But all the evidence seems to suggest that even Japan's phenomenal success is more a result of economic necessity than any other single factor. Indeed, most of Japan's technological advances do not stem from its homogeneity but, rather, from the careful observations it has made of its American ally. While a common ethnic and religious heritage may have its advantages, the energy and competitive spirit created in a diverse America has far outweighed the benefits of uniformity in the past. If we can learn to take advantage of these strengths now, we can use them to win again in the future.

AMERICAN HERITAGE

America offers many other advantages that also foster competitiveness. It has the world's largest consumer market, the most extensive and sophisticated communications systems, a free press, a massive and universal education system, an extensive transportation network, an expansive heartland that supplies food and natural resources, and, above all, a heritage of innovation, social mobility, and entrepreneurial spirit.

Sometimes we forget about this heritage, or simply take it for granted. But most visitors from abroad who spend some time in the United States are inevitably surprised to find the country so extraordinarily class-free and democratic, its people daring to think great thoughts. Even the Swiss, Japanese, and Germans, renowned as tireless workers, are amazed at how hard Americans work and how economically and socially mobile we are. Here, everyone has the chance to pursue the highest goals, even though we may not all begin at the same starting line or achieve the same degree of success. And the stigma of failure is greatly diminished because most Americans are truly forgiving: starting over again at a new job or setting up yet another new business is always a possibility. Such attitudes stimulate productive activity and competition.

All has not been perfect in U.S. business, however. In the 1970s, inflation, high taxes, government controls, OPEC, and other culprits—from inflexible unions to social engineers—slowed our traditional gains and diminished our historic advantages. Though much has been done to restore our competitiveness, many remedial measures still need to be taken. Deregulation, fairer and lower taxes, reduced inflation and interest rates have helped, as has focusing more attention on some basic educational deficiencies. But more remains to be accomplished in each of these areas and elsewhere. And how well we do in improving the competitive environment today will affect our ability to be productive, competitive, and profitable in the years to come.

It is still possible to use America's natural and man-made advantages to your benefit in becoming a more successful competitor. The examples we have provided here have shown how others have tried and succeeded. People, investment, quality, ingenuity, and hard work are the elements common to all their stories. And if you follow their lead, you too can enjoy the success that lies ahead.

CORPORATE CASE STUDIES IN PRODUCTIVITY

The thing that scares me now is that we know
our true costs, but competitors don't.
—Richard P. Simmons
President and CEO

ALLEGHENY LUDLUM CORPORATION

Computerized Cost Measurement System, Aided by
Nonfunctionalized Management Organization, Helps Achieve
45 Percent Productivity Improvement

THE PROGRAM

Allegheny Ludlum makes 126 standard grades of stainless steel and over 400
varieties. Throw in exotic alloys, and the number rises to the thousands. All told,
the company has 26,000 recipes for making specialty steels, and it changes 1,000
each month. A coil can go through thirty phases of rolling, annealing, pickling,
rerolling, and polishing in two or three plants before it's finished.

A ton of specialty steel can take five times more man-hours to produce than a
ton of carbon steel. So company-wide managing of costs is a continuing necessity.
Five years of number crunching went into developing a data base sophisticated
enough to model every specialty process. Today, the system can track every
nickel's worth of nickel from furnace through twelve-ton coil for each of 30,000
coils of steel scheduled around the company's seven plants.

This information system also evaluates every order and schedules its production. Each order is analyzed by size, profit margin, and production allocations,
all aimed at assuring profitability and overall efficiency. Then the computer
allocates each order's slot in a production run, and tracks the process using bar
code tags and readers.

EVALUATION

Allegheny Ludlum has managed to string together more than forty consecutive
profitable quarters. At 14 percent, its return on total capital is equal to that of any

major domestic steel producer, and its debt has been reduced to 35 percent of capital.

Over the last six-and-a-half years, the number of tons produced per man-hour has increased 45 percent, while in the last four years the quality index has risen 30 percent. Workers at the New Castle, Indiana, plant produce a ton of stainless sheet every four man-hours—perhaps 50 percent faster than any competing plant. Overall, the company produces over $250,000 in sales per hourly employee.

Productivity improvement at Allegheny Ludlum is largely due to its sophisticated computerized cost-control system, but its success has been aided by management teams organized along six product lines—not by function. Each team is responsible for achieving specified profit targets rather than sales or productivity quotas.

Contact: Hubert W. Delano
Director—Corporate Communications
Allegheny Ludlum Corporation
Pittsburgh, Pennsylvania 15222–5479
(412) 394–2800

Less fare, more care.

AMERICA WEST AIRLINES

New National Carrier Ties Employee Stock Ownership,
Job Cross-Utilization, Fuel-Efficient Aircraft, and a Hub City
Operation to Achieve High Employee Morale and Productivity

THE PROGRAM

As one of the new low-fare carriers established after deregulation of the airline industry, Phoenix-based America West began with a "clean slate" in developing its organizational and productivity programs.

Its plan for success had four central precepts: establish a dominant position at Phoenix Sky Harbor International Airport, utilizing it as a gateway to the West; fly modern, fuel-efficient aircraft; create high employee productivity and morale through employee ownership, incentive stock options, and profit sharing; and offer high-quality service at low fares.

America West now schedules more than 170 daily departures from Sky Harbor Airport, double the number of its closest competitor. By using its dominant position in Phoenix and Las Vegas, where it operates nearly 100 daily flights, the airline has developed a "superhub" concept, offering modern, uncongested terminals that makes these cities attractive alternatives to the other "gateways" to the West, such as Denver.

The entire America West fleet consists of seventy Boeing aircraft, most of them 737s, considered the most fuel-efficient passenger planes in the world. Boeing 757s and Boeing de Havilland Dash 8s allow the carrier to access both long- and short-distance markets, and make its fleet one of the world's most modern. By the end of 1988, its fleet is expected to be *the* most modern.

All new America West employees are required to purchase company stock equal to 20 percent of their first year's base salary. The stock is discounted 15 percent from the market value, and a low-rate company financing program is available. An incentive stock option program has also been developed for employees. And whenever the company produces a profit, employees are rewarded with profit-sharing checks, distributed on a quarterly basis. Profit-sharing amounts are determined by each employee's base salary and seniority in the company.

Every one of America West's Customer Service Representatives (CSRs) is trained to work sixteen different positions. A typical workweek will find a CSR taking reservations, issuing tickets, loading baggage, and operating as a flight attendant. This cross-utilization program increases each CSR's knowledge of the total operation and creates an extremely productive employee.

A number of innovations have also been introduced to increase customer satisfaction. Among the amenities: complimentary cocktails, assigned seating, large overhead storage bins, free copies of *The Wall Street Journal* and *USA Today*, and full interline services. A frequent-flyer program, FlightFUND, rewards those business travelers who do not have the luxury of taking advantage of America West's lowest fares, which require advance purchase. In addition, the "Careliner" bus service takes passengers to and from Terminal III at Sky Harbor Airport to Scottsdale and Mesa, Arizona, while the "Phoenix Club," a luxurious VIP lounge, offers members the rest and relaxation required for every trip, whether business or pleasure.

EVALUATION

America West inaugurated service on August 1, 1983, with three aircraft serving five cities. Today, it is the nation's tenth largest carrier serving forty-five destinations with more than 7,000 employees. Passenger enplanements are near the 1 million mark for each month, and operating revenues reached almost $650 million in 1987.

Contact: Daphne Dicino
Director, Corporate Communications
America West Airlines
222 South Mill Avenue
Tempe, Arizona 85281
(602) 784-5729

In today's highly competitive environment, all companies are looking for some type of edge. We look for this edge in productivity improvement.

—*William Schneider, Director*
Industrial Engineering Group

AMERICAN SEATING COMPANY

Cost-Reduction Teams Use Committee Process to Set Productivity Goals and Provide the Plans and Operating Leadership to Achieve Them

THE PROGRAM

The American Seating Company is the world's largest producer of seats (for stadiums, schools, buses, etc.) and a major manufacturer of office furniture. Its sales exceed $100 million a year.

For a long period of time, American Seating had used informal committees in production, engineering, and other parts of the company to look for ways to improve productivity. In 1982, however, the president decided to formalize the process into the Cost Reduction Committee System, expanding it to all areas of the company (e.g., inventory control, returned goods) and making it an integral part of American Seating.

These cost-reduction committees contained four to ten supervisors and managers drawn from different areas of the company, and each committee member was required to attend a training session to become familiar with other departments and to learn techniques that would help him or her make the most of the committee process. Each committee established its own goals for productivity improvement and put a precise monetary value on the savings it hoped to achieve. Once these goals were set, the committee then attempted to accomplish them as it saw fit, purchasing new equipment, for example, or redesigning a production line. Committee chairpersons also met on a regular basis with a steering committee to discuss progress, problems, setbacks, and other matters of mutual concern.

EVALUATION

The Cost Reduction Committee System was ended at American Seating in November 1987 and will not be used again. Instead, each functional area in the company has now been made responsible for establishing and meeting its own cost-reduction targets.

The committee system, however, did accomplish three important objectives: (1) it helped save the company money; (2) it cross-trained managers from different departments; and (3) it created a new team spirit by showing employees how to work together on a project.

It also helped bring about significant—and permanent—productivity increases. A robotics committee, for example, had been looking into equipment improvements for some time. So the company purchased a robotic mig welder which increased productivity over 50 percent in the welding portion of the operation.

As a result of such decisions, the company realized millions of dollars in savings since 1982, savings of $3.58 million in 1986 alone.

Contact: William Schneider
Industrial Engineering Group
American Seating Company
901 Broadway, N.W.
Grand Rapids, Michigan 49509
(616) 456–0600

There are two basic motivating opportunities for independent Amway distributors. The first is selling products and services, and the other is an opportunity to develop a sales organization by sponsoring new distributors.

—Amway Corporation Brochure

AMWAY CORPORATION

Dual Opportunity Reward System Motivates Independent Sales Distributors and Helps Company Achieve $1.6 Billion in Sales

THE PROGRAM

All direct-sales organizations face the challenge of how to keep the motivation of their sales force high and commissions equitable. At the Amway Corporation, a sophisticated reward and recognition system does just that, and it has helped Amway's one million distributors worldwide chalk up sales revenues of more than $1.6 billion a year.

What is even more surprising is that Amway's entire sales force consists of independent business people, not employees of the company, who come from all walks of life. Their income from Amway is based on a commission that averages 30 percent if they sell the company's products at the suggested retail price (though they may, in fact, sell at any price they want) and a performance bonus.

The Performance Bonus is calculated on the basis of two sets of numbers: Point Value (PV), which does not change, and Business Volume (BV), a dollar value that changes with inflation. At the present time, 1 point of PV is equal to approximately $1.56 BV.* The greater the total PV sold by a distributor, the greater the percentage of bonus paid on Business Volume.

Monthly PV	Performance Bonus
100	3% of BV (Business Volume)
300	6%
600	9%
1000	12%
1500	15%
2500	18%
4000	21%
6000	23%
7500	25%

*Note: For purposes of illustration, the round figure of $2.00 is used in the example.

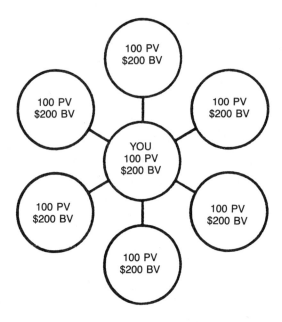

Total Monthly PV 700
Total Monthly BV $1,400

9% Performance Bonus ($1,400 x 9%)	$ 126
You Pay	−$ 36
You Keep	$ 90
30% Basic Discount (on $200)	+$ 60
Monthly Gross Income	$ 150
Annualized Gross Income	$1,800

A distributor who sells 100 PV (or $200 BV) in one month, for example, and averages 30 percent in commissions, receives a total income of $66 for that month (30 percent x $200 + 3 percent Performance Bonus on $200).

Amway distributors can also earn additional income by finding and sponsoring other distributors. In fact, the company will pay each distributor a special bonus based on the total sales of all new distributors sponsored. Once a distributor starts sponsoring others, however, it is his or her responsibility to pay their Performance Bonus. The potential income that can be earned by a sponsoring distributor is calculated in the example below.

(Remember, however, that this is only an example. Sponsoring distributors earn more or less based on their monthly performance, and as the chart above shows, the performance bonus can reach as high as 25 percent.)

Besides their monetary compensation, Amway distributors are recognized in many other ways. With rising sales volume comes eligibility for awards and designations, and those who truly excel can even win trips and cars. Any time anyone achieves a new sales plateau, his or her picture is also featured in the Amway magazine, the *Amagram.*

EVALUATION

Amway's unique compensation, reward, and recognition system has helped total company sales grow from $500,000 in 1959 to $1.6 billion today. And it is flexible enough to allow the company to focus on different business objectives as conditions in the marketplace change. At the present time, for example, the company is introducing a number of new product lines and services to emphasize the many ways current Amway distributors can increase their income. The result is that in recent years, the company's sales per distributor have increased dramatically. These enhanced sales opportunities also provide an additional incentive for any would-be distributors who wish to own and operate a business of their own.

Contact: Kimberly Bruyn
Manager—Public Relations
Amway Corporation
7575 E. Fulton Road
Ada, Michigan 49355
(616) 676–7196

We can make a Mac every twenty seconds.
—Apple Management

APPLE COMPUTER, INC.

Just-in-time Inventory Control and Materials Flow Systems
Provide Improved Quality, Increased Productivity, and
Lower Cost in High-Tech Manufacturing Plant

THE PROGRAM

Since November 1983, Apple's MacIntosh computer plant has manufactured
over 200,000 machines. One reason for this enormous productivity is the fact that
the MacIntosh factory has implemented a just-in-time inventory system to control
materials flow. Before parts are distributed to their production locations, they are
categorized and recorded in the factory's computer control system, and all purchased materials are tested for quality as they enter the plant.

Each part is classified into one of two categories: bulk parts and small parts.
Bulk parts include video displays, chassis, housings, and power supplies; small
parts are items like integrated circuits and microprocessors. Bulk materials are
distributed to the proper work stations by an overhead parts delivery system,
while automated storage and retrieval systems handle the small parts, distributing
them to the work centers where they are needed. If workers need more parts, they
can put their empty part-totes on a conveyor that automatically sends them back
for refills.

Other parts are carried to work stations by robot-like automated vehicles
that are battery-powered and can freely maneuver around the factory floor.
Workers can request parts from the robotic system from their work station
terminals.

EVALUATION

Apple's materials flow system has reduced inventory costs while maintaining a steady flow of parts into the work areas where they are needed. Compared to a manual assembly line, this automated system has achieved a remarkable number of efficiencies, including:

1. a 53 percent direct labor saving
2. a 17 percent overhead saving
3. a 20 percent total cost saving

Today, Apple is automating even further to improve its production process. But when we asked about the newest improvements that have been made, the company's managers would only respond with a sales pitch for their newest Mac—a clear affirmation of the old rule: sine emptor nullum negotium—without a customer, you are out of business. This combination of the traditional free-enterprise ethic and cutting-edge technological improvements makes Apple one of the better competitors in what is perhaps our most competitive field.

Contact: Catherine Mason
Public Relations and Communications
Apple Computer, Inc.
48105 Warm Springs Boulevard
Fremont, California 94538
(415) 659–6476

BEA is seeking to diminish the separation of "decision" and "execution" to counter the tendency to fragment work typical of larger firms.
—Corporate Philosophy

BEA ASSOCIATES, INC.

Fund Management Firm Retains Key Money Managers and Achieves Spectacular Growth Through Participative Compensation and Centralized Operational Support

THE PROGRAM

Participative management was adopted at BEA to promote individual achievement and provide the effective collaboration necessary for implementing investment strategies.

Eight asset fund managers are the company's core managing group. Assisted by one back-up manager, each is responsible for his or her client's investments, and performance is measured monthly by the return on investment of the funds under management. Periodically, portfolios are adjusted for risk and diversification, with the results reviewed by the other fund managers.

Each year, BEA's fund management performance is analyzed by a research unit that determines where value was added and by whom. Then all eight fund managers study the report and indicate in writing what they think their own and their associates' compensation should be. These votes are collected and read aloud (only the vote results are made public), and a simple average of the votes is used to determine a fund manager's total compensation. The system eliminates politicking, encourages communication among peers, allocates rewards where achievement is clear, and publicly reinforces desired performance.

To avoid growing "islands" of staff around each fund manager, operational and clerical support units have been centralized. Headed by only one administrator, these units provide support for all eight fund managers.

EVALUATION

Investment management is a business noted for independent thinkers and high turnover. But in the last thirteen years, BEA has lost only three money managers. The assets it manages have grown about 30 percent annually, from $100 million to $6 billion, even though the number of its employees has increased just 67 percent, a payroll increase that represents only 3 percent of the company's growth in discretionary assets.

BEA's integrated approach to participative management may prove to be useful in other companies where talented individuals require close collaboration to achieve superior results.

Contact: Emilio Bassini
Administrator
BEA Associates, Inc.
One Citicorp Center
153 East 53rd Street
58th Floor
New York, New York 10022
(212) 310–0254

Everyone's looking for an edge these days: something to improve margins, raise product quality, or keep employees interested in their jobs. Many Beatrice companies have found that edge—through productivity improvement.
—Beatrice Productivity Guidebook

BEATRICE COMPANIES, INC.

Giant Manufacturer Installs Total Productivity Program at 150 Profit Centers and Achieves $50 Million in Savings

THE PROGRAM

When Beatrice Companies decided to institute a five-step productivity improvement program in 1979, Step One was to create a basic awareness through the company of the need to improve productivity. This was accomplished largely by including productivity presentations at management meetings, by contributing articles on productivity to employee newsletters, and by developing special audio-visual materials for use in employee gatherings. The company's chairman of the board also sent a letter to each division president emphasizing the message that Beatrice was serious about improving its overall productivity.

Step Two in the program was employee education. This was accomplished through a series of two-and-a-half day Productivity Improvement Workshops directed toward profit center presidents, directors of manufacturing, and productivity coordinators. The workshops focused on four major areas:

• managing for productivity improvement;
• involving employees;
• developing tools, techniques, and case studies on productivity improvement; and
• developing specific action plans.

Step Three, recognizing employee achievement, placed great importance on creating the proper incentives for change. This was accomplished through a subsidiary program called Uncommon People, Uncommon Goals, which allowed each profit center to decide where it would like to focus its productivity efforts, what goals it would set, and what kind of awards it would give out.

Each time goals are met, you'll be eligible for awards. The exact type of award will be decided by your company. Typical awards range from free coffee and rolls every day for a period of time to company-sponsored special events for employees and their spouses—like a concert or a ball game.*

Beatrice also developed its Star Award for those managers whose units recorded exceptional improvements in productivity. Hung in the manager's office for all to see, the Star Award was the company's "biggest sales tool in selling productivity," according to Manager of Productivity Improvement Mike Bremer.

Measuring the results of the program in actual dollars saved was Step Four of the productivity improvement effort, while Step Five was integrating productivity into the company's overall business plan. "For the program to sustain itself, productivity goals had to tie into the company's profit goals," says Bremer. And this was done chiefly at the local level, where each profit center was allowed to identify its own productivity objectives, establish the programs it needed to meet them, and calculate its expected results.

EVALUATION

Beatrice's five-step productivity improvement program produced impressive results, especially between the years 1981 and 1985.

Year	Profit Centers Participating	Savings
FY 81	$ 13	$ 7,000,000
FY 82	140	$27,000,000
FY 83	150	$40,000,000
FY 84	N.A.	$50,000,000

At Beatrice, productivity improvement is not an option, it is a necessity. And management knows that the key to any successful improvement effort is the people who make it happen and succeed.

Ted E. Olson, previously a Beatrice operations vice president, reports that Beatrice management recognized that employees were the key to success in becoming more competitive:

Motivated employees mean better productivity. Better productivity means more jobs, higher demand for products made, increased sales, greater profits and, therefore, higher pay and better fringe benefits for all.

Note: Beatrice Companies, Inc. was purchased in April 1986 by BCI Holdings Corporation in a leveraged buyout. The company has since reorganized under a new management team.

---

*Beatrice Productivity Guidebook

Especially when money market funds were new and we had a lot of explaining to do, a computerized phone service's help was enormous.

—Wayne Sibly
Former Chairman & CEO

CALVERT GROUP

Computerized Telephone System Creates Satisfied Customers for Financial Services Organization

THE PROGRAM

When the Calvert Group started offering a popular new money market mutual fund to investors, the company soon found that the traditional telephone system it was working with was woefully inadequate to meet its growing business needs. Reaching the company was frustrating and difficult for customers, and the morale of employees was being adversely affected by the constant barrage of complaints they were hearing.

After carefully evaluating all the new technologies now available, the company decided to purchase a Rolm MCBX with Automatic Call Distribution. The MCBX balances the work load of telephone representatives by automatically apportioning incoming calls based on the number of calls waiting, the length of time they have been on hold, and the average length of time each call takes to answer. The system can also be programmed to divert incoming calls to "flex team" employees during peak periods, thereby decreasing waiting time and increasing customer service. The hard data collected by the system over time can also be used to determine staffing needs.

EVALUATION

The Calvert Group was so pleased with the performance of its Rolm MCBX, that the company has decided to upgrade the system to incorporate "voice response."

This technology allows a customer to indicate what kind of service or information he or she needs without talking to a Calvert employee. Merely by pushing a button on a touch-tone phone, a customer can place an order, check an account balance, or find out the daily yield on a money market mutual fund.

For management at the Calvert Group, there is no question that the use of a computerized telephone system has increased the number of its satisfied customers and improved employee morale as well. Staff members no longer have to spend time handling routine inquiries, and can devote themselves fully to address the more substantive concerns of their clients. The system has allowed the company to accommodate a substantial increase in customers without having to hire additional staff, and as an unexpected benefit, the company has also been able to reduce its overall telephone costs.

Contact: Mike Watkins
Shareholder Servicing
Calvert Group of Funds
1700 Pennsylvania Avenue, N.W.
Washington, D.C. 20006
(202) 951-4800

It is an historic breakthrough, not only in labor-management relations, but also in meeting the national need to improve productivity.

—Los Angeles Times

CERTIFIED GROCERS OF CALIFORNIA LTD.

Labor-Management Plan Rewards More Productive Warehouse Workers with Time Off and Extra Pay

THE PROGRAM

At the outset, Certified Grocers sought to increase productivity and profits in its multi-billion-dollar wholesale grocery business by targeting three specific areas: (1) warehouse operations, (2) accounting, and (3) data processing. Quality circles were formed in all three areas and their efforts were coordinated with a steering group chaired by company senior vice president Don Gross who met regularly with a broad spectrum of employees. A standing committee that included truck drivers and traffic superintendents was also set up in the transportation department.

The warehouse quality circle was the first to come up with a workable suggestion for productivity in its area. It recommended that an incentive system be established in which certain rewards—either extra pay or time off with pay—be granted to those workers whose performance exceeded the average work performance or an agreed-upon standard.

Local Teamsters union 595 played an important part in setting the warehouse work standards. It brought in a team of experts to work with the company's production engineers in determining a fair standard against which actual work performance could be measured and bonuses paid. Senior Vice President for Distribution Bob Walz also agreed that certified employees would be strongly motivated by the opportunity to earn paid leisure time, so he decided to make paid time off a key reward in the program and worked together with both top management and the rank and file to develop acceptance performance criteria and an attractive reward schedule.

The performance standards that were eventually accepted are based on engineer evaluations of how much work can be accomplished by an average worker within the existing work environment. Past performance achievements played a role in devising these performance standards, but it should be noted that they are *not historical* averages that are raised whenever the company's overall productivity takes a leap. This avoids penalizing steady workers who, for whatever reason, are unwilling or unable to increase their productivity.

This is how the system works: Every employee earns .45 minutes of paid time off for every hour of work performed that measures between 100.5 and 114 percent of the engineering based standard. If the employee produces at a level exceeding 115 percent of the standard, he or she receives .60 minutes per hour for every percentage point above 100.5.

That means that an employee who works thirty-five hours at 115 percent of standard earns 304.2 minutes (35 x .60 minutes x [115 - 100.5]) of time off with pay. This time off can be accumulated for one quarter but must be used up during the following quarter. If the employee desires, he or she can choose a financial reward instead that is equal to one-half the time pay for the earned time off.

The system set up at Certified works in such a way that efficient and productive workers are rewarded, but slow workers are not penalized as long as they stay within 10 percent of standard. If a worker drops below 90 percent of standard, however, Certified does apply disciplinary measures that include verbal and written warnings, and temporary and permanent dismissal. But there are also features to the system that allow an employee to remove these "black marks" permanently from his or her record.

EVALUATION

During the first year it was installed at Certified, the new incentive program helped the company increase productivity more than 15 percent and save more than $2 million in payroll costs. And these savings have increased every year since then. The company has been able to encourage above-average performance without paying overtime, hiring more workers, or paying more fringe benefits for the extra work done. In addition to that, it has experienced a dramatic decrease in absenteeism, employee turnover, and labor grievances.

The program is simple and basic and can be replicated almost anywhere there is a measurable production standard. Other food retailers, such as Ralph's, Von's, and Safeway, have implemented similar programs. It is the kind of incentive system that has all the ingredients for success: It has the support of labor and management, it offers rewards that motivate people, and it is fair.

Contact: Robert Walz or Jerry Friedler
Certified Grocers of California LTD.
2601 South Eastern Avenue
Los Angeles, California 90040

The goal of creating a corporate identity was to develop closer ties between the company and its employees.

—Aubrey Cole
Senior Vice President

CHAMPION INTERNATIONAL

$4 Billion Conglomerate Develops Corporate Philosophy of Employee Involvement to Help Improve Productivity

THE PROGRAM

Each of the formerly independent companies that merged to create Champion International had its own corporate identity, but Champion had no image that employees could relate to. This lack of identity did not create a sound environment for productivity improvement, thought CEO Andrew C. Sigler, so he decided to develop a corporate philosophy called The Champion Way. In addition, Sigler decided to ask employees for their suggestions on how to cut costs and improve productivity at Champion's paper-pulp and wood operations.

As envisioned by Sigler, The Champion Way is a seven-step approach to creating a new corporate culture. It includes:

1. *The Champion Way Statement*—an outline of the goals and objectives of the company that clearly tells everyone where everyone else is headed.

2. *Communication*—the use of an Involvement Team Approach to create broad, open lines of communication. These teams, which are strictly voluntary and self-organized, look for production problems in their work areas and attempt to eliminate them. "Any financial savings achieved by the team are a side benefit," says Senior Vice President Aubrey Cole. "The main idea is involvement." The company is also running a series of ads nationwide, more for the purpose of achieving a unified corporate identity than for any marketing reasons.

3. *Training and Development*—a set of comprehensive programs for managers and future managers. One program, Managing for Excellence, is a "fast-track" course for middle managers with high potential that focuses on financial

and human resources training. Several other specialized programs are also available for foremen who want to improve the way they supervise front-line workers.

4. *Work Environment Tangibles*—a commitment to improving working conditions in Champion's plants and offices.

5. *Work Environment Intangibles*—ways to build trust between labor and management. Since the company's union has not totally embraced The Champion Way, management is trying to keep the union well informed of what it is doing and why as a means of building confidence.

6. *Organizational Structures*—attempts to structure the organization of company businesses in a manner consistent with both product and people.

7. *Employee and Community Activities*—full support to those who involve themselves in extracurricular activities either at the company or in their community.

The Involvement Team Approach has been used primarily to address production problems at Champion's paper-pulp and wood operations. When a specific problem is identified in any area of the mill, the area supervisor begins recruiting a team by identifying eight to ten interested lower-level managers and line employees. Normally, the first-line supervisor serves as team leader, but company coordinators and facilitators are also used to explain the benefits of team participation and lead the newly assembled team through problem-identification techniques.

Once operational, a team meets at least once a month to discuss the nature and cause of the problem and to identify possible solutions. When the team has reached a consensus, its solution is presented to the area supervisor, who must decide whether or not to implement it. If the supervisor's response is positive, the team has the option of staying together to work on other problems.

EVALUATION

As a result of The Champion Way, employee morale at Champion International seems to be higher and the team concept is spreading quickly throughout the organization. Since December 1983, twenty-three teams have been formed in the paper-pulp division, saving the company $1 million at the Pasadena mill alone. The company estimates that the teams helped save $4 million in the entire paper division the first year they were set up.

Contact: Aubrey Cole
Senior Vice President
Champion International
One Champion Plaza
Stamford, Connecticut 06921
800–892–5912

*People need to be recognized; everyone needs to
feel important or feel as if they also have
contributed to our success. This all sounds
corny, but it can work.*

—*Hoyt Parmer*
Former President

COMO PLASTICS

Plastics Company Improves Labor Relations and Profits Using
Teamwork and Owner Involvement

THE PROGRAM

Como Plastics, a maker of molded plastic framing used by manufacturers of high-
technology equipment, had a history of poor labor relations during the 1970s;
strikes in both 1973 and 1976 reflected the turmoil. So when C. W. Jackson
purchased the company in 1980, he decided to approach management matters
differently. He installed a new management team and imposed a new management philosophy: teamwork.

By 1988, the philosophy of employee involvement had become a way of life, as
did Total Quality Control and the just-in-time production system. Management
now takes an active position in being not only the leader but also the disciple of
the employee involvement religion. Words like "survival" are included in every
expression of the company's philosophy and management style and the active
approach highlights "cost management" rather than "cost accounting."

How did Como do it?

1. At the outset, specific goals were established and articulated:

   a) Plant utilization would be raised to 80 percent—(even though the industry average was only 72 percent).

   b) Pre-tax profit margins would be raised to 8 percent (the industry average—6 percent), and a system for paying bonuses based on achieving profit
targets would be established.

2. Personalized labor-management relations were made a necessary ingredient in any effort to move the company ahead. It started with the first-ever

company Christmas party with gifts and entertainment. Then an annual picnic was made a company tradition, as were Thanksgiving turkeys and Christmas hams. Eventually it became apparent to everyone that the company's management did view its work force as consisting of real people.

3. Sharing information was made a key step in motivating employees and getting their views on important company matters. Once a month now, a member of management meets with all staff personnel to discuss the company's production problems and financial performance during the previous month. Twice a month a member of management meets with twenty members of the production staff where the same information is released, but in a more condensed form. According to the president, these regular meetings make everyone "feel more a part of the whole thing."

In addition, the chairman and the president have breakfast with twelve or thirteen employees on a monthly basis, where anything is open for discussion— from production techniques and profits to new product lines and retirement benefits. The company also encourages the formation of quality circles and has a record of implementing about 75–80 percent of all circle recommendations.

EVALUATION

After Como Plastics changed hands and employee involvement was made an integral part of the corporate culture, sales volume more than doubled, from $8 million in 1980 to $17 million in 1983, while profits increased 800 percent in the same period. In addition, a new union contract that both sides felt was equitable and fair was signed in 1986 after only three days of negotiations and four meetings. Labor grievances, which reached up to thirty-five a year before 1980, were totally eliminated.

Today, labor-management relations at Como Plastics are generally excellent, and the teamwork environment permits previously unthinkable goals to become a reality. Employees have truly become part of the company team and they know it.

Contact: Philip S. Newton
President
Como Plastics
2860 North National Road
P.O. Box 387
Columbus, Indiana 47201–0387
(812) 372–8251

It has always been my firm belief that employees contribute to the growth of a company as much as capital, and employees should, therefore, participate in that growth.

—Warren Braun
President and CEO

COMSONICS INCORPORATED

Inc. 500 Growth Company Combines ESOP and Employee Participation to Meet Goals

THE PROGRAM

When Warren Braun started ComSonics in 1972, it was his idea that all employees should share in the responsibility of running the company as well as in reaping the financial rewards from it. He chose two methods to achieve his goal: participatory management and employee ownership.

His first step was to provide a vehicle that would help employees share in the company's success—an Employee Stock Ownership Plan (ESOP). But "after the first year," says Braun, "I found myself with a disaster on my hands. It was as if the employees had been handed a stone rather than the tools to work for greater profits." One of the reasons the ESOP was failing was that employees did not understand what an ESOP was or how it worked to their benefit.

To overcome this obstacle, the company undertook a massive educational program to instruct everyone in the basics of stock ownership, stock value, and the part employees can play in improving that value.

Working in tandem with the ESOP program is a participatory management system based on the principle of "operation by objective." Each company, division, and employee at ComSonics is given a set of goals and may attempt to achieve them in whatever way that is deemed best. Today, strategic planning is done not only at the top levels of the company, but also in the middle and at the bottom. "Such a system takes flexibility by the chief executive officer," says Braun. "They will make some mistakes, and at times you just want to dump the whole thing."

To provide a forum for the exchange of ideas, managers and supervisors each hold two meetings a month. The first deals with operational issues, analyzing the current budget, where the company stands in making the budget, the upcoming budget, and what improvements and gains have been made and can be made. The second meeting involves longer-range planning, looking at goals, projections, and expectations.

Then, once a month, there is a "free-for-all" meeting where supervisors and managers leave their titles outside the door; anything is open for discussion. "When these meetings first began," says Braun, "there was a lot of finger pointing. But today everybody is more concerned with the company's goals and objectives and how they can best be met." It is important to note that all these meetings take place with the Chief Executive Officer *not* in attendance, helping to make sure their discussions remain free and uninhibited.

In 1986–87, the company bolstered its commitment to worker participation by setting up an Employee Advisory Committee and allowing direct employee voting in board meetings. As a result, any thinking about policy decisions and the setting of goals does not stop at the supervisory level but continues down throughout the company. Because all employees are stockholders, even production workers are considered one of the four levels of management and are expected to help in the decision making process. For example, when the diagnostic and repair areas were faced with the problem of too little space, too little time, and too much to do, workers set up a committee to look at possible solutions and decided to add a third shift with a 12 percent pay differential. Although this meant that many workers (including some committee members) would lose their overtime, it was still considered to be the best solution to the problem for the company as a whole.

EVALUATION

In 1987, overall corporate profits at ComSonics increased by 300 percent. Over the past five years, the company has been on *Inc.* magazine's list of the 500 fastest growing companies in America, its sales volume increasing during the period more than 260 percent. Braun evaluates the program this way: "They [the programs] cost a bundle in time, they cost a bundle in people effort, but I tell you, they do work and they work beautifully. They actually sing the way they they work."

Contact: Warren Braun
President and CEO
ComSonics, Incorporated
P.O. Box 1106
Harrisonburg, Virginia 22801
(703) 434-5965

I should have been more aggressive. If I had known what we would save through this program, I would have been willing to spend more money on it earlier.

—John Bretherick
President

CONTINENTAL INSURANCE COMPANY

Measuring White-Collar Productivity in a Large Insurance Company Proves Possible, but Modifying Standards to Meet Organizational and Technological Change Proves a Greater Challenge

THE PROGRAM

Continental Insurance operated its domestic property and casualty business through forty branch offices throughout the United States, and various analyses had shown that branch expenses were ranging from 3 to 13 percent of total premium income. In an effort to control and standardize these branch expenses, the company developed a Productivity Performance Index (PPI) using existing branch office data.

Three different measurements are totaled to calculate a branch office's PPI. First, to evaluate staffing levels and compare branch office efficiencies, a Productivity Indicator weights transaction costs according to difficulty for each processing unit in the branch. Second, the ratio of transaction expenses to premium income is calculated to evaluate relative costs of processing. Finally, service timeliness is measured by figuring the average number of days required to process different insurance instruments. When added together, these measurements produce the PPI: an accurate indicator of a branch office's productivity, expenses, and effectiveness that can be calculated merely by compiling data that is routinely forwarded to the company's main office.

Using the PPI, the company's Productivity Research and Development Department has produced a 200-page manual of procedures, called the "Branch Office Productivity Guide," that has been used to bring about significant technological and organizational changes within the company. New standards to meet new procedures are currently being developed, with implementation expected in little more than a year, and the measurements that result from these changes will be incorporated in a new PPI.

EVALUATION

In its first year of using the PPI, Continental increased its productivity (work load compared to staffing) by 18.4 percent, raised its service levels by 12.5 percent, and reduced its branch expenses by 5 percent. Relying only on attrition and early retirement, its total branch office staff fell 20 percent. By 1986, however, new sales techniques and office procedures had to be introduced to deal with dramatic changes in the marketplace, so old standards had to be put on hold while new ones were developed. But the company believes that a new PPI standard can be developed within two years and that it will continue to help in generating additional productivity improvements.

As Continental Insurance has shown, the creative transformation of data into meaningful measures of white-collar productivity is a difficult area to work in, yet it is one of the primary areas of opportunity for achieving productivity improvement today.

Contact: John Dwyer, Vice President
Agency Group Operations
Continental Insurance Company
1 Corporate Place South
Piscataway, New Jersey 08854
(201) 981–8535

The only dumb question is the one you do not ask.

—Dana Folk Saying

DANA CORPORATION

Diversified Vehicular Components Manufacturer Designs
Outstanding Productivity Program Based on Communications,
Full Disclosure, and Participative Management

THE PROGRAM

Communication is a key aspect of the total productivity environment at Dana
Corporation.

Every employee is scheduled to meet with a senior manager at least once a
year, and each Dana facility displays posters with tear-off sheets that are pre-
stamped and pre-addressed to the chairman of the board. Employees are encour-
aged to write to the chairman if they have a question, a problem, or just want
information. Once a quarter, the chairman sends a letter to every employee's
home outlining his personal views on the company's future, its market share, and
other issues.

During the last seven working days of each month, operating results for every
unit and division within Dana are made available, and employees also receive
information monthly on the corporation's overall performance and how it com-
pares to the previous year. There is even an 800 number shareholders and employees can call for current information on the company; and questions or suggestions may be left at the end of the taped telephone message.

With no more than five levels of management and a management-by-walking-
around style, face-to-face communication has largely replaced memo writing.
Extensive job rotation also helps build internal people networks, while promotion
from within provides additional incentives for growth. To further promote participation, even budgets are prepared from the bottom up, and all production

108

Forty Thoughts

Remember our purpose—to earn money for our shareholders and increase the value of their investment

Recognize people as our most important asset.	Provide autonomy.	Promote identity with Dana.	Insist on high ethical standards.
Help people grow.	Encourage entrepreneurship.	Make all Dana people shareholders.	Focus on markets.
Promote from within.	Use corporate committees, task forces.	Simplify.	Utilize assets fully.
Remember—people respond to recognition.	Push responsibility down.	Use little paper.	Contain investment—buy, don't make.
Share the rewards.	Involve everyone.	Keep no files.	Balance plants, products, markets.
Provide stability of income and employment.	Make every employee a manager.	Communicate fully.	Keep facilities under 500 people.
Decentralize.	Control only what's important.	Let Dana people know first.	Stabilize production.
		Let people set goals and judge their performance.	Develop proprietary products.
		Let people decide where possible.	Anticipate market needs.
		Discourage conformity.	Control cash.
		Be professional.	Deliver reliably.
		Break organizational barriers.	Do what's best for all of Dana.
		Develop pride.	

procedures are developed by those who will actually use them.

Gainsharing plans are used in approximately thirty-five of Dana's manufacturing plants and distribution centers. Whenever productivity increases are registered in a particular plant or center, each person there receives a cash bonus.

Much of Dana's innovative management style has been summed up in what are called the "forty thoughts" (see chart at left).

EVALUATION

Dana is now one of the most successful manufacturing companies in the country. Its constant dollar sales per employee have doubled over the last decade, in part because increasing profits through productivity planning has been made an integral part of its corporate culture.

Contact: Robert Cowie
Vice-President, Public Affairs
Dana Corporation
P.O. Box 1000
Toledo, Ohio 43697
(419) 535-4500

The one word that will have a great impact on labor-management relations and on how productivity responds: recognition!
—Daniel C. Boyle
Vice President and Treasurer

DIAMOND INTERNATIONAL
(Diamond Fiber Products as of December 1984)

Small-Gift Club Recognizes Workers Who "Do Their Job Well," Reducing Absenteeism 42 Percent and Creating Employees Who Feel Appreciated

THE PROGRAM

Diamond International created "The 100 Club" at its egg carton plant as a way of recognizing employees for their contribution to the company.

The idea that the company needed a formal recognition and reward system came about after a grievance committee meeting between the union and management. Daniel C. Boyle, then personnel manager, realized that nothing was being done for the majority of employees who simply did their jobs well. "They don't get the ego massage they need," Boyle pointed out, and his perception was confirmed by an employee survey conducted in 1980. The results of the survey revealed that

- 65 percent of all employees felt they were not treated respectfully; and
- 79 percent felt they were not rewarded for a job well done.

In addition, employee grievances had risen to 150 a year and work days lost to absenteeism to 3,303.

To rectify the matter, Boyle created The 100 Club in February 1981. The Club rewards employees with points for doing their job well. Points are awarded on an objective basis (e.g., 25 points for 100 percent attendance), and when an employee accumulates 100 points, he or she formally becomes a member of The 100 Club, receiving a blue nylon jacket with a patch signifying membership. Any points earned over 100 can be used to purchase gifts. "The gifts earned with points are not particularly expensive,'' says Boyle, "and are well within the workers' purchasing power. But the basic premise of The 100 Club is not to 'buy' increased profits and productivity with lavish gifts but to demonstrate management's interest and concern for its employees.''

EVALUATION

To measure the long-term impact of the program, Diamond International conducted another employee survey in 1983. Its results revealed that

- 86 percent felt management considered employees to be either "important" or "very important"; and
- 77 percent felt they were adequately rewarded through "recognition" from their supervisors.

At the same time, it was calculated that worker output had increased 16.5 percent, absenteeism had declined 42 percent (with savings of $114,462 in 1982), and worker grievances had dropped to about forty a year.

As a result of these findings, Diamond International decided to install The 100 Club in three of its other plants. Though installation took about ten weeks and start-up costs totaled nearly $100,000 in the following eighteen months, the company ended up saving over $5 million and experienced a 14.5 percent increase in productivity.

In the past four years, Daniel C. Boyle & Associates, Inc., has begun approximately sixty similar programs around the nation in all types of firms, from manufacturing to service organizations, and at the present time, all programs are on or ahead of schedule. Though the Diamond International Corporation is technically no longer in existence—Boyle and his partner, Robert E. Arnold, bought and renamed the company Diamond Fiber Products, Inc. in 1984—the 100 Club continues to generate productivity growth of about 2.3 percent a year at Diamond Fiber with corresponding improvements in attendance and industrial safety. And many of the same results have been duplicated at other businesses where The 100 Club has been installed, such as Owens-Corning Fiberglas Corporation, Marcus Printing Co., Schulz Electric Co., Nestle Foods Corp., and Heekin Can, Inc.

The 100 Club has shown to be an effective tool in improving labor-management relations, worker morale, and organizational productivity. It has also proved, according to Boyle, that "the American worker, by way of the Diamond worker as an example, is second to none.''

Contact: Daniel C. Boyle
Vice President and Treasurer
Diamond Fiber Products, Inc.
P.O. Box 627
Thorndike, Massachusetts 01079
(413) 283–8301

Involved Donnelly employees achieve success.
The Donnelly Ideas program is alive and well—
this program was critical to our success.
—Dwane Baumgardner
President

DONNELLY CORPORATION

Midwest Auto Supplier Uses Employee Ideas to Achieve
Competitive Edge

THE PROGRAM

The Donnelly Management System, which has taken thirty years to evolve, does
not lend itself well to being picked apart in piecemeal fashion. Yet even though all
its parts are integrally related to one another, that does not mean other companies
cannot draw valuable ideas from it.

The Donnelly system is based on four basic principles:

1. An organization must build structures and processes so that employees
have the opportunity to participate in ways that make them feel valued as individuals.

2. The system must be based on competence.

3. The customer must be the focus in all planning and problem solving.

4. Productivity must be consistently rewarded.

Donnelly uses a modified Scanlon plan to reward individuals or groups for
productivity improvements. Though many Scanlon plans focus primarily on
suggestions, cost reductions, and bonuses, Donnelly also looks for ways to
further promote employee participation. It does this primarily through work
teams, equity teams, and the Donnelly committee.

Work teams. The cornerstone of the Donnelly Management System, work
teams are groups of employees who report to one boss and have a common
mission. Everyone in the organization belongs to at least one work team—
including the company president.

Supervisors are the "linchpins" of the work team approach. Their membership on both subordinate teams and peer-level teams allows for information to flow freely up and down the organization. Work teams also have overlapping responsibilities, and try to concern themselves not just with their own objectives, but with the goals and accomplishments of the entire organization.

Equity committees. There are five equity committees in the corporation whose members consist of one representative from each work team, each member serving a two-year term. Equity committees deal with personnel policies, wage levels, grievances, and other similar matters, and all their decisions must be reached by unanimous vote. If a decision affects only one area in the company, the committee has the authority to implement it, but if the decision affects more than one area, it must be passed on to the Donnelly Committee.

Donnelly Committee. Made up of fifteen voting members—thirteen from the equity committees, one representative from production supervision, and the president—the Donnelly Committee includes four resource members who do not have voting privileges. As in the equity committees, all decisions made by the Donnelly Committee must be unanimous.

EVALUATION

While scores of suppliers to the auto industry are declaring bankruptcy, Donnelly has garnered a bigger share of the market, introduced new products, and increased sales substantially. And this increase in sales has not been limited just to domestic markets. Donnelly now supplies one-third of the mirrors that grace all cars imported from Japan.

Bigger company profits also mean employee payouts at Donnelly, and profit sharing bonuses in the last few years have averaged 8 percent.

Several years ago, a Ph.D. candidate spent some time at Donnelly to determine whether or not the company really does benefit from its unusual management approach. Taking into consideration all the company's organizational development costs—staff salaries, meeting time, program expenses, training, etc.— he credited half the company's productivity improvements to the Donnelly Management System. He calculated that over a seven-year period, the company's return on investment was 220 percent.

Contact: Kay L. Hubbard
Corporate Manager of Human Resources
Donnelly Corporation
414 East 40th St.
Holland, Michigan 49423
(616) 394–2217

The RMS cannot directly be transferred to another agency, even one with somewhat similar programs. However, the concept and techniques used in this project can be applied to a great many case-processing operations.

—Donald Kull
Consultant

FARMERS HOME ADMINISTRATION (FmHA)

Computerized Resource Management System Helps Government Agency Allocate Funds and Personnel Efficiently

THE PROGRAM

A work measurement system at FmHA was in place by the mid–1970s to monitor the activities of its 11,000 employees in 1,950 county offices, 250 district offices, and 46 state offices. But the system was complex, time-consuming, and subject to individual reporting inaccuracies, and productivity was calculated by comparing current performance to a previous base period. It was felt that a better system could be developed.

The Resource Management System (RMS) that evolved from the previous work measurement system started on the county level, then went on to include district and state offices. Its goals: simplification, greater accuracy, and more timely generation of productivity measurements. A one-page, end-of-the-month report submitted by each office was the heart of the RMS (though the one-page county office report has since been combined with another data collection report, while district and state office reports have been automated).

The RMS differs from the previous work system used at FmHA in that productivity is now measured against national average work standards for loan processing, which are periodically updated. Only time actually spent in processing loans is used to calculate the productivity index (PI), since travel and training times vary widely due to the different geographical locations of agency offices. And only aggregated office data are used—eliminating individual reporting inaccuracies, reducing compliance efforts, and facilitating the preparation of office budget and staffing needs.

The PI is calculated by dividing total earned time (calculated from loan output) by net program hours (reported by offices) and multiplying by 100.

EVALUATION

Using RMS data, the FmHA has been able to calculate more accurately the resources it needs to meet the demand for agency services and to justify budget and staffing requests. The RMS has also proved useful as a tool for employee position classification and other personnel management purposes. Recent efforts by the Office of Management and Budget to promote productivity improvements are being addressed by the agency through the use of RMS data.

The FmHA now has the technical capability to provide agency-wide management reports solely from information residing in its automated systems. It is also in the process of developing a new Work Management System that will enable the agency to eliminate the current field reporting burden, improve information accuracy and accessibility, and eliminate redundant computer processing.

Because of the RMS, the productivity of individual offices in servicing their loans can now be compared against national averages to assist in the efficient budgeting of money and staff throughout the FmHA.

Contact: Maxine J. Lewis
Information Resources Management Division
Farmers Home Administration
U.S. Department of Agriculture
South Agriculture Building
14th & Independence Ave., S.W.
Washington, D.C. 20250
(202) 447-9296

Our focus has shifted from defense detection to defect prevention and a drive to satisfy the customer.

—*John Manoogian*
General Manager

FORD MOTOR COMPANY

U.S. Automobile Manufacturer Finds Continuous Quality Improvement the Key to Customer Satisfaction

THE PROGRAM

Like it or not, many American auto manufacturers in the 1970s were losing their reputation for competitive quality in products and services. The reason: companies like Ford traditionally relied upon a "reactive" quality control system, where the emphasis was on finding and fixing quality problems as quickly as possible rather than on seeking ways to prevent them. Defects and breakdowns, even if fixed expeditiously, were costly and inefficient and were no longer acceptable to the American consumer.

As foreign competition continued to intensify, it became increasingly more obvious that the find-and-fix approach had to be replaced. Ford was finding it more difficult to market cars against higher-quality foreign imports, and was spending more and more to redo what should have been done right the first time.

The company established a quality assurance office charged with the task of putting high quality back into Ford's products. The first priority was to confirm and publicize the CEO's support for the effort. "Unless you receive the support of the CEO and the president," says then Executive Director of Product Assurance John Manoogian, "believe me, you're not going to get to first base."

Under the direction of the new quality assurance office, the company provided training for all managers that focused on finding opportunities for improving quality in production, and a 171-point checklist was introduced at each assembly plant to pinpoint problems that needed corrective action.

All employees began using the pilot Escort program, which organized workers into reliability teams, where they were trained to understand how quality control helps build a better car. A separate employee involvement program was also used to complement the Quality is Job One (Q1) effort.

Design and assembly engineers were trained to work together to use statistical process control techniques in measuring production variances. Since quality costs can increase as product characteristics vary, Ford invested heavily in advanced technologies like CAD/CAM, flexible manufacturing systems, and automation to reduce product variability and the probability of error.

The Q1 program was also established to recognize suppliers who maintain high quality standards. Job preference was given to those with the best quality records, and longer contracts were awarded to those with a continuing commitment to quality in the materials they supply Ford. In addition, the quality commitment performance program (QC-P) was launched to rate dealer service.

EVALUATION

In 1987, the quality improvement effort at Ford was as much alive as it was in 1983. Now institutionalized in the company's "Mission, Values and Guiding Principles" and in a policy letter entitled "Ford Total Quality Excellence," a key part of the effort has been the realization that productivity improvement can only come from quality improvement.

In recent years, greater emphasis has also been placed on Total Quality Excellence (continuous improvement of all processes, not just in manufacturing) and on understanding the "voice of the customer."

Since 1980, the Ford team has improved domestic car and truck quality by more than 60 percent, proving that "doing it right the first time" is what achievement in industry is all about.

Contact: Frederick Z. Herr
Vice-President, Product Assurance
Ford Motor Company
Rotunda Drive at Southfield
P.O. Box 1522-A
Dearborn, Michigan 48121
(313) 337–5200

*We've learned that the plan and its
implementation need to be uniquely suited to
your particular business and, as importantly, the
specific financial objectives you have for it. . . .
There is no magic, just good knowledge of your
needs.*

—Dr. Charles E. Cheeseman
Senior Scientist

GE'S DAYTONA SIMULATION AND CONTROL SYSTEMS

Robots Build Simulation and Control Systems Faster and Better

THE PROGRAM

Ten years ago computer-generated visual image systems were a high-tech special-ty. Built mostly by hand, only about a dozen were produced each year. Since then, however, the demand for such systems has increased 700 percent, and GE needed to find a way to increase production while still maintaining its high quality standards.

GE's solution was to design its new Daytona plant as "the factory of the future." It contains a two-armed, light-assembly robot that can trim, form, and insert components, sense and discard damaged or inferior parts, and reduce programming time when adapting to minor variations in the printed wire board designs.

With its two x-y-z arms, the Daytona robot is capable of seven different motions, and special features permit it to transfer assemblies on and off and to gauge insertion force to prevent damage to components. Both arms operate simultaneously and do not have to stop for loading or unloading. A human operator can remove individual boards when completed and has only to supply parts and boards in response to the robot's needs.

EVALUATION

The robot at GE's Daytona plant has significantly improved the manufacturing precision of visual image systems and greatly increased GE's production capa-

bilities. It can assemble boards three-and-a-half times faster than a human operator and its sensing capabilities have reduced errors and board defects by 42
percent.

Contact: Ken Kilner, Manager
General Electric Company
Daytona Simulation and Control Systems
1800 Velvia Avenue, Building Five
P.O. Box 2444
Daytona Beach, Florida 32015
(904) 258-2511

*One other old dog has learned new tricks. We've
moved in computers, lasers, robots, and a
highly advanced handling system. It's still an
old building from the outside, but inside those
meters are pouring out.*

*—Jules Mirabal
GE Technology Manager*

GE'S METER AND CONTROL BUSINESS DEPARTMENT

GE Converts Old Factory to High Productivity Using
Computerized Materials Handling and New Addition on the Roof

THE PROGRAM

At GE's meter plant in Somersworth, New Hampshire, increased production requirements had outstripped plant capacity. The need for outside warehouse space was imminent, but there was nothing available within a reasonable
distance. To make matters worse, an inefficient materials transport system between floors that used freight and passenger elevators was very time consuming.

GE took the existing multi-floor structure and built a new addition on the roof.
A sophisticated materials handling system—one equally as efficient as those used
in single-floor plants—was designed to include three automated storage systems
and two conveyor networks. Raw materials, work-in-process, and finished goods
are now handled separately, and materials can be requested from storage through
data terminals on each assembly floor. An executive computer controls all three
storage systems as well as the conveyor network that services the finished goods
and work-in-process systems.

Special design features have also been added to increase productivity and
space utilization. In the finished goods system, for example, a conveyor loop with
multiple spurs interconnects the adjacent unit-load and mini-load systems and
interfaces with an automatic lift, which carries finished goods to the second floor.

Work-in-process materials are also controlled by computer. Inventories are
called up when needed for assembly, and the appropriate tool boxes are distributed to the assembly floors by the conveyor network and automatic lifts.

EVALUATION

The new computerized retrieval system at GE's Somersworth plant creates 40,000 square feet of storage space in the old building, 10,000 square feet more than would have been gained if an adjacent warehouse had been added—and at a lower cost. Before the new system was installed, 75 percent of a stockkeeper's time was spent traveling between storage sites, but now materials are brought over automatically. In addition, the computer system maintains a file on material location to keep track of the distribution and receipt of stock for operators.

Contact: William McDonogh, Director
Employee and Community Relations
GE—Meter and Control Business Department
130 Main Street
Somersworth, New Hampshire 03878
(603) 749-8500

Our locomotive plant in Erie is almost seventy-years old. We spent $300 million giving that plant an electronic heart transplant. I wonder if people think of brand new factories when you talk about automation. Well that's not necessarily the case.

—*Joseph Podolsky*
Plant Manager

GE'S ERIE LOCOMOTIVE PLANT

GE Refurbishes 70-Year-Old Industrial Plant, Increasing Productivity over 240 Percent

THE PROGRAM

When it came to locomotives, GE realized that it was slowly being squeezed out of the market. Its existing manufacturing technology was antiquated and its competitors were already using high-tech equipment to produce a superior product. To meet the competition head on, GE decided that nothing less than a total redesign of its locomotive manufacturing system would do.

At the company's seventy-year-old locomotive plant in Erie, Pennsylvania, a motor frame flexible machining system that uses nine unmanned machine tools was installed, as was a parts-load station, and an automatic material transport system. Some of the more innovative features of these new technologies included:

1. computer-directed carts that automatically distribute parts to each machine station;

2. cutting tools that can be changed by numerical controls;

3. coolant and chips that can be automatically removed; and

4. new machines that are so adaptable that they can be substituted for one another within the system.

The plant's steel plate burning facility, which fabricates more than 25,000 tons of steel plate parts per year, was also fully automated. It featured:

1. CALMA interactive graphics system that automatically displays different-shaped parts specifically designed to fit each plate more precisely;

2. a burn machine that can be programmed so that a crane with magnetic lifters automatically delivers two-ton plates from the storage facility to the machine table; and

3. a computerized numerical control plasma-arc burning system that can cut two plates at once using four cutting torches (and is capable of cutting up to 150 inches per minute).

EVALUATION

As a return on its initial investment, GE saw overall productivity at the Erie plant increase by more than 240 percent with significant improvement recorded in both product quality and consistency. The company has since added another unit to the plasma burning system to handle two-thirds of the total plate burning load. This has had the effect of doubling the plant's output, providing a 100 percent increase in labor productivity and a savings in material costs of up to $400,000 a year.

Contact: Joseph Podolsky
Plant Manager
General Electric Company
Erie Locomotive Plant
2901 East Lake Rd.
Erie, Pennsylvania 16531
(814) 875–3957

People working at night pay a price in terms of mental and physical health. If we can make their lives easier, why shouldn't we?
—Preston Richey
Operations Manager

GREAT SALT LAKE MINERALS & CHEMICALS CORPORATION

Shift Schedule in Tune with Workers' Circadian Rhythms Boosts Productivity, Lessens Fatigue in Round-the-Clock Operation

THE PROGRAM

During peak seasonal production at the Great Salt Lake Minerals & Chemicals Corporation, work was performed around the clock in three shifts. Employees changed to the previous shift every seven days, but changing that often had unwanted side effects: one in three workers was reported falling asleep on the job.

Preston Richey, manager of operations, decided to conduct an experiment in conjunction with Dr. Charles Czeisler and the Center for Design of Industrial Schedules at Harvard University, an expert on human "circadian cycles" (or internal "body clocks"). They divided the work force into two groups: one was to change schedules every seven days, as before, while the other was to change only every twenty-one days. Knowing that most body rhythms tend to lengthen in the absence of environmental time cues, they also changed the direction of rotation forward for all employees—from day to swing to night shift.

Under this new scheduling system, complaints about schedule changes dropped from 90 percent to 20 percent among those in the group that rotated every twenty-one days. Turnover, absenteeism, and family problems all declined, while health and morale improved and productivity increased 20 percent. The entire work force was soon changed to the new twenty-one-day schedule. "Four years ago, our goal was 1,000 tons of potash per day," says Richey. "Now 1,500 tons is average with the same work force."

The company has also spent considerable amounts of time and effort to educate supervisors on how to measure productivity and how to share this information in visual form with hourly workers so that they can gauge their own output on a weekly or daily basis.

EVALUATION

The new schedule rotation program continues to have widespread acceptance among employees at the Great Salt Lake Minerals & Chemicals Corporation. Though potash operations were curtailed due to flooding of the pond system, all other operating areas in the company continue to show a 3 to 7 percent productivity improvement each year. Since one in four men and one in six women in the U.S. labor force work on variable schedules, this experiment highlights an unrecognized phenomenon that may have major implications for American industry.

Contact: M. J. Reynolds
Vice-President, Operations
Great Salt Lake Minerals & Chemicals Corporation
P.O. Box 1190
Ogden, Utah 84402
(801) 731-3100

We try to remember to demonstrate that every job is important and each individual, in carrying out his function well, is an important contributor.
—Hewitt Associates Philosophy

HEWITT ASSOCIATES

Benefits Consulting Firm Designs Program for Employees Juggling Work and Parenting Responsibilities

THE PROGRAM

As a consulting firm that designs progressive compensation and benefits programs for other companies, Hewitt Associates decided to help its own employees who are working parents by providing the following assistance:

1. *Maternity Return Options*. In some cases, associates who have recently had a child are allowed additional unpaid time off or can return to work on a part-time basis for a limited period. If there are special needs, the associate can discuss the situation further with a manager to decide whether the same or a similar job would be available after an extended leave, and whether the job is one that can be covered during the interim period by someone else.

2. *Reimbursement for Overnight Babysitting*. Hewitt often provides reimbursement for overnight babysitting costs to associates who must be out of town on business overnight. Those who qualify must be either single parents or have a working spouse who is also out of town on business. This reimbursement does not include care provided by a live-in sitter or relative.

3. *Salary Conversion Limit*. Associates are permitted to convert as much as $4,800 from their yearly salary to a Flexible Compensation spending account to cover health-care and dependent-care expenses.

4. *Sick Child Care*. Hewitt has negotiated an arrangement with area hospitals that allows associates to reserve vacant pediatric beds when their children are not well enough to go to school. Costs vary from $30 to $40 and are the parent's responsibility. This program provides an additional option for parents whose day-care facilities cannot accommodate sick children.

5. *Parent's Helper.* The company employs a "Parent's Helper" to act as a reference and referral resource for employees with children. The Helper collects, evaluates, and shares information on child-care providers, dry cleaners, housekeeping agencies, etc., and cuts down on the time working parents have to spend investigating these services.

EVALUATION

Working parents, especially single parents and parents in dual-income families, suffer high levels of guilt and anxiety today about not spending enough time with their children and not spending enough time at their jobs. They feel strongly that it is their responsibility to do well at both parenting and working. In this regard, any psychological support, practical timesavers, and information resources that can be offered are greatly appreciated.

As a benefits consulting firm, Hewitt has developed a program that demonstrates creativity and resourcefulness in responding to the vast changes taking place in society, in the workplace, and in the integration of work and family life. It has shown that increased employee morale is achievable at a relatively low cost. And though it is hard to put a dollar figure on the benefits of the program, no one doubts that it has improved the company's ability to compete.

Above all, being more sensitive to the needs of working parents provides a way of showing that the company cares about its employees.

Contact: Peter E. Friedes
Chief Executive
Hewitt Associates
100 Half Day Road
Lincolnshire, Illinois 60015
(312) 295–5000

By establishing a far-reaching goal and getting people to feel in their gut that the goal was reasonable, we felt some serious movement would begin to occur. We also knew the close linkage between high quality, lower costs, and increased productivity would lead to other beneficial results for the company.

—John Young
CEO

HEWLETT-PACKARD COMPANY

Total Quality Control Program Achieves Ten-Fold Increase in Reliability at Major Electronics Firm

THE PROGRAM

At Hewlett-Packard, as much as 25 percent of its manufacturing assets were tied up simply in mobilizing "reactions" to quality problems. Though quality standards were high, improvements were needed if the company was to maintain its leadership position in the electronics industry. So a new quality program was developed that went well beyond the quality circle concept to Total Quality Control (TQC).

The first step the company took in that direction was to establish a goal: to improve reliability by a startling 1,000 percent. Management felt that by setting such a difficult-to-reach objective employees would focus more on changing their basic approach to work and less on improving their old ways of doing things. "Perfection is the goal" became the company slogan and customer satisfaction the test of achievement.

Second, all senior managers were trained in quality assurance techniques. Doing it right the first time was the principal lesson to be learned.

The third area of the program focused on stimulating employees to increase productivity. Newsletters, informal meetings, training classes, and over 1,000 quality teams were set up to accomplish this feat.

The fourth step involved instituting a computerized management information system. Research employees were guaranteed unlimited access to needed information data bases for experimentation, and programs were developed to track rework and parts failure data.

The fifth step was to encourage vendors and suppliers to participate in the

TQC program. Involving the supplier, it was thought, would ensure quality parts and a quality product.

Finally, the TQC approach was expanded from manufacturing to other areas within the company, such as inventory control and accounts receivable.

EVALUATION

As a result of the TQC program at Hewlett-Packard, quality and productivity have improved dramatically.

- Service and repairs on desktop computers have dropped 35 percent through improved design and manufacturing techniques.
- Overall production time has been reduced—lowering the cost of the company's two most popular oscilloscopes by 30 percent—and product defects have declined substantially.
- Major improvements have been recorded in the quality of parts supplied by vendors participating in the TQC program.
- Inventory costs fell from 20.5 percent of sales in 1979 to 13.8 percent of sales in 1987, leading to savings of $542 million.
- Overdue receivables dropped to $218,000 within two years, meaning that $434,000 less is now invested in the company in the form of uncollected funds.

In 1987, the approach was also extended to Hewlett-Packard's TQC strategic planning and implementation process. Management believes that this move may bring about even more breakthrough results than the application of TQC to any area of the company so far.

Contact: Julie Holtry, Manager
Corporate Quality Marketing and Communications
Hewlett-Packard Company
3172 Porter Drive
Palo Alto, California 94304
(415) 857–4884

HONEYWELL INC.

Participative Productivity Programs Proliferate Producing
Prodigious Profits

THE PROGRAM

From its initial Twin City Suggestion Plan for hourly workers—which has been in
continuous operation since 1942—to the dozens of new programs and techniques
now in operation, management in this labor-intensive organization has long
focused on increasing productivity. Most recently, since 1987, the emphasis has
been put on improving quality and productivity in white-collar areas.

Honeywell's new "Winning Edge" program is a multi-tiered system of communications that enables employees to understand better how their contributions
relate to the whole of the company. The Strive for Error Free Performance
(STEP) program stresses quality and the need to meet customer requirements
precisely, while Value Analysis is being promoted in overhead and staff areas to
measure productivity gains over time. The Aerospace and Defense Group's
Productivity and Quality Center provides guidance and consultation throughout
the company, encouraging productivity through both better communications and
internal competition. Extensive use is also being made of work-flow and input-
output analysis.

More than 1,100 quality circles are now in place throughout the company, and
the original suggestion plan has been extended to non-hourly workers paying up
to $2500 per suggestion.

EVALUATION

All these new programs at Honeywell have helped to produce an atmosphere in
which employees work actively to improve productivity. The introduction of

extensive automation and robotics has ignited little or no resistance from the work force. Energy use in the last decade has been reduced 34 percent, while total output has increased 65 percent. And $29 million dollars has been saved through suggestion systems alone since 1975. In a recent survey, 70 percent of Honeywell's work force agreed with the statement that productivity improvement is everyone's responsibility.

Contact: Arnold M. Weimerskirch
Director, Corporate Quality
Honeywell Plaza
2701 Fourth Avenue South
Minneapolis, Minnesota 55408
(612) 870-6781

Skilled, responsible management and superior productivity are inseparable. We are entering a far more demanding era requiring greater professionalism in management. Tomorrow's manager, in addition to being technically qualified in his or her field, must be a respected, people-oriented leader skilled in the latest techniques of behavior science and sound business practice.

—Robert Ranftl
Retired Corporate Director

HUGHES AIRCRAFT COMPANY*

Managers Learn How to Improve Personal and Company Productivity in One-Day Training Session

THE PROGRAM

Where *does* one find a "skilled, responsible manager"? Hughes Aircraft believes they are not found, but created. That is why management development has been a crucial part of this company's operations for many years.

Not long ago, a one-day management seminar was designed at Hughes by Robert Ranftl "to develop not only understanding of productivity but a dedicated commitment to productivity improvement throughout our entire management team." At the outset of each seminar, Ranftl, now retired, would point out that "good managers do not fit the same mold—each one must use his or her own unique style—and that the purpose of the seminar was the "sharing of insights and a shopping list of ideas and productivity tools."

Now given hundreds of times, the seminar is today divided into four modules, each concentrating on a different facet of productivity. The first module reviews the "Anatomy of Productivity": Why is productivity important? What affects productivity? How does one evaluate productivity? And most importantly, how does one improve productivity? This kind of basic, primer approach is used so that the managers can return to their own unit or department after the seminar and have an immediate positive impact on the grass-roots level.

The second module in the seminar looks more closely at managerial and organizational productivity, focusing on the most common factors that aid or inhibit productivity improvement in companies across the nation. It also looks at

---

*Now a division of GM.

the roles management must play in dealing with counter-productive factors, placing special emphasis on the role of leadership. "True leaders bring out the best in people and organizations," says Ranftl. "This is largely because leaders elicit strong positive emotional reactions, and because people tend to fulfill their needs and grow under effective leadership."

The third module deals with personal productivity, identifying a number of ways to combat counter-productive tendencies, while the fourth module identifies specific ways to improve productivity at Hughes. Here, the seminar group is divided into smaller subgroups, each of which brainstorms ways to overcome counter-productive factors within the organization. Their suggestions are then passed onto senior management, so that those in the upper echelons of the company can learn what their subordinates want to see done.

EVALUATION

The seminar approach that is used at Hughes Aircraft to develop managers may be somewhat unique, but it has shown to be highly effective. And the popularity of the program continues to grow. It never fails to help managers to identify productivity inhibitors and to discover new ways to eliminate them.

Contact: Mr. Robert M. Ranftl
Corporate Director (Retired)
Engineering and Design Management
Hughes Aircraft Company
P.O. Box 49892
Los Angeles, California 90049
(213) 471-1804

Humana is state of the art in terms of cost control and plans to be state of the art in terms of providing medical technology.

—Robert Irvine
Manager

HUMANA INC.

Central Computer Purchasing System Results in Savings of $85 Million over Three-year Period

THE PROGRAM

When Humana first began to expand rapidly, its managers could see that duplications in billing, purchasing, and staff could become very costly. So they decided to install a mainframe computer that would link all terminals throughout the hospital system and to implement a cost-reduction program that focuses on three major areas.

Billing: All patient bills and insurance forms are now fed through telephone lines at night to the main data processing center in Louisville. Insurance companies and other health care service vendors receive all their information—batch-style—from this central facility.

Purchasing: The mainframe computer keeps track of supply levels at each Humana hospital, and all medical equipment is purchased through a central office. Buying supplies for 17,000 hospital beds allows Humana to take advantage of substantial volume discounts.

Staffing: Almost 60 percent of any hospital's operating costs are attributable to staffing. So at Humana, staffing requirements are based on departmental work load, as indicated by an automatic statistical gathering process that provides an analysis of the skill levels needed on any particular day. Taking into consideration the number of patients being treated, the computer then calculates each hospital's daily staffing requirements. A reserve corps of employees is on call twenty-four hours a day, seven days a week, and a special effort is being made to use lesser-skilled employees as often as possible and to reserve more highly skilled employees only for those times when they are truly needed.

In addition, Humana is constantly evaluating the efficiency of its support system to make sure its professionals are being properly served at all times. The financial and practical feasibility of contracting out some services—such as biomedical engineering or food plans—to other industry experts is also being evaluated on a regular basis.

EVALUATION

Centralizing computer operations at a large health care organization can prove to be highly cost-effective. At Humana, the new billing procedures help speed up the receipt of revenues, and the purchasing program is expected to save $85 million in three years.

Humana also estimates that its effort to closely monitor staffing levels gains the company a 5 percent cost advantage over other hospitals. For Humana, this equates to a savings of approximately $35 million a year.

Contact: George Atkins
Vice-President, Public Affairs
Humana Inc.
P.O. Box 1438
Louisville, Kentucky 40201–1438
(502) 580–1439

Even though our products are untouched by human hands, you still have to have humans. You're going to have a better quality product as long as the humans maintain the machine and do it properly.

—Nancy Mikaelian
Executive Vice President

HURON MACHINE PRODUCTS, INC.

Manufacturer Implements Employee Training Program to Realize Maximum Yield from FMS Investment

THE PROGRAM

While other businesses were having problems making ends meet during the 1982–83 recession, Huron Machine Products was investing heavily in Flexible Manufacturing Systems (FMS), Computer-Aided Design/Computer-Aided Manufacturing (CAD/CAM), and Computerized Numerical Control (CNC) systems to aid in its own design and manufacture of FMS components. But these high-precision manufacturing systems led Huron into a "people trap": the systems' sophistication exceeded the company's ability to use them efficiently. Some training was being provided by distributors, but Huron felt that to fully utilize these "new age" products it would have to address the human operator factor.

So the company introduced a work team concept into its Flexible Manufacturing System. The objective: to motivate workers to improve their productivity by helping them understand what the new technology could do for them.

These work teams, which have been used for over four years now, are set up according to work areas, and meetings are run by regular employees who have been trained as facilitators. A facilitator's job is to coordinate the meetings, help generate ideas, mediate conflicts, and encourage positive thinking. Statistical quality control techniques are reviewed during the meetings, charts and graphs are used to illustrate machine productivity and product quality, and intricate analyses are made to help plan short- and long-term production periods.

The basic rationale behind the program is to increase the flow of communication between management, the work force, and the computerized machinery. But the program also is being used to document and review the productivity levels of these new, high-tech manufacturing systems.

EVALUATION

Huron's Flexible Manufacturing System operates twenty-four hours a day, seven days a week using three twelve-hour shifts, each shift working four days on and four days off. After the introduction of the system in 1983, operators were able to improve the productivity of the company by 22 percent over 1982. Since then, Huron has experienced continued productivity improvement and expects still further improvement in the years to come.

Another benefit: due to a combination of efficiency and attrition, Huron has been able to reduce its work force requirement by 33 percent. As jobs are displaced due to increased efficiencies, employees are routinely retrained and reassigned. Attrition can be filled with re-trained and re-assigned personnel.

With its computer-controlled manufacturing systems, the company has also eliminated the need for rework and reduced re-set-up time because any mistakes in initial set-up are caught during simulated trial runs. Over the years, both the workers and engineers have learned to develop and utilize high-level skills to manage the company's sophisticated systems productively.

Contact: David H. Lindemann
President
Huron Machine Products, Inc.
228 Southwest 21 Terrace
Fort Lauderdale, Florida 33310
(305) 587–8292

Our goal is to make Intel the best administered company and be able to prove it. We want to work smarter, not harder.
—Intel Productivity Program

INTEL CORPORATION

Work Simplification Technique Helps Reduce Bill-Paying Process by 93 Percent and Doubles Manufacturing Efficiency

THE PROGRAM

Back in 1979, more than 50 percent of Intel's work force consisted of support personnel, and management decided that if the company were to remain profitable and competitive, it would have to open the black box of administrative productivity. The first step: the creation of a continuous, selective, quantitative system to focus on improving productivity.

That decision led to the development of the company's Administrative Productivity Program. It consists of four parts:

1. the Administrative Productivity Indicator (API);
2. work simplification;
3. a work load management system; and
4. methods for monitoring progress.

The core of the program is the belief that all jobs can be measured, and the API is the method Intel uses for measuring output in an administrative area. It does this by first identifying a basic work unit, then determining the output of that unit over a specific period of time (the number of letters typed in a day, for example, or the number of phone calls handled in a week). The API is calculated by dividing the number of hours worked into the total output, and this figure can then be compared with other benchmark measures.

Work simplification is another important aspect of Intel's productivity improvement strategy. It entails looking at each step in a particular job process and determining which are unnecessary and can be eliminated. The steps that remain are then reassembled in the most efficient way possible. Work simplification has allowed Intel's literature department to streamline its bill-paying procedures from 198 steps to 14, a 93 percent reduction.

The third part of the Administrative Productivity Program is a work load improvement system that helps managers determine exactly how much labor is required to complete a certain task. Its effectiveness is based on three simple questions: What do you do? How often is it done? How long does it take? By answering these questions as thoroughly as possible, a manager should be able to calculate easily the labor requirements for a specific job.

Each division within Intel is allowed to determine which part of the productivity program it wants to undertake based on its own circumstances. But the basic approach is the same throughout the company: identify the problem, brainstorm solutions with staff, decide on a plan, obtain support from all affected personnel, implement the plan, and monitor its progress and effectiveness.

EVALUATION

During the first four years of the Administrative Productivity Program at Intel, 42 percent of the administrative staff had become involved in at least one part of the program, while 17 percent had experienced all four. Since then, the program has been extended beyond the administrative staff, and certain refinements have been made, including separating the program into two segments, one focusing on operational effectiveness and the other on efficiency.

Productivity improvement as a result of the program has not been uniform throughout the company, but every division has achieved at least some positive results. The Materials Department, for example, has developed a corporate-wide program that has been generating savings of about $1.27 million a year. And the company as a whole doubled its manufacturing output from 1986 to 1987.

Contact: Gary M. Homan
Corporate Productivity
Corporate Productivity
Intel Corporation
5200 NE Elam Young Parkway
Hillsboro, Oregon 97123
(503) 696–5730

*Quality will determine who wins in the
competitive banking market.*

—*William Latzko*
Irving Trust Consultant

IRVING TRUST COMPANY

Bank's Statistical Quality Control Procedures Lower Error Rates
by as much as 70 Percent

THE PROGRAM

In banking, quality is measured by the way in which services are delivered to the
bank's customers. But each day, thousands of clerical tasks are performed in a
bank, and thousands of errors are made. The need to correct these errors before
they reach the customer led Irving Trust Company to develop a statistical quality
control approach to "taming the paper tiger" called QUIP (Quality Improvement
Program).

QUIP helps improve production quality in the bank's clerical systems by
measuring the four "costs" that each system has to manage: (1) Appraisal Cost—
the cost of checking or verifying that the work has been done correctly; (2) Internal Failure Cost—the cost of wasted effort and any rework; (3) External Failure
Cost—the cost incurred by the next system from receiving incorrect input; and
(4) Prevention Cost—the cost of quality control efforts. By focusing specifically
on reducing Internal Failure Costs, managers who use QUIP have found that they
can have a significant impact on effectively reducing all the other costs.

Supervisors who have been trained in QUIP sample the output of each of their
clerks regularly and keep an ongoing record of the quality of the work being
produced. If an error is discovered during sampling, a supervisor attempts to
"fix the problem, not the blame." Then, using these individual output files and
statistical analysis, the supervisor can determine the precise capability of each
clerical system. Comparing individual output to these standards helps supervisors
focus on those areas of individual performance that need improvement.

EVALUATION

In general, the QUIP system has resulted in a drastic reduction in internal failure at Irving Trust, eliminating 50 to 70 percent of the mistakes that had previously been made. There has also been a definite impact on external failure rates: by reducing the number of mistakes made in the first place, fewer mistakes are reaching the customer. This has resulted in substantial savings in out-of-pocket expenses and has improved customer relations. The latter, while intangible, can nevertheless be quite real, especially when quality is improving to such an extent that senior management is receiving direct feedback on it from customers. The bank is now working on a new strategy that can better measure how the quality of its work is living up to customer expectations.

Contact: Michael Shayne, Director
Equipment and Quality Engineering
Irving Trust Company
1 Wall Street
New York, New York 10015
(212) 815–2246

*Throughout its history, the JLM Committee has
served to open lines of communication that are
grounded in the belief that new attitudes, trust
and risk-taking can result in a better
understanding and appreciation of each other's
responsibilities and concerns.*
                              —Nicholas A. Fidandis
                                           Chairman

JOINT LABOR MANAGEMENT COMMITTEE, RETAIL FOOD INDUSTRY

Structured Cooperation Between Union and Management
Engenders Trust, Stability, and Foresight

THE PROGRAM

The need for better cooperation between labor and management was recognized in the retail food industry during the last era of wage and price controls, from 1971 to 1974. The present Joint Labor Management Committee (JLMC) of the Retail Food Industry was established in 1974 by volunteer representatives from both management and labor, partly as an outgrowth of the Tripartite Wage and Salary Committee of the Cost of Living Council. As now constituted, the JLMC includes members from the three largest unions in the industry and thirteen supermarket companies. These companies range in size from the largest operating in the United States and Canada to mid-size and smaller regional chains, which altogether employ more than 400,000 workers represented by the three member unions. The JLMC is charged with improving collective bargaining, preventing unnecessary strikes, promoting long-range stability, and encouraging open and high-level communication on various issues affecting the retail food industry.

The JLMC is funded annually by both the unions and corporations, whose chief officers form the Executive Committee. Under the direction of an impartial chairman, the Executive Committee determines the issues to be addressed and sets policy guidelines for implementation by a Steering Committee consisting of the corporate VP's of labor and industrial relations and their union counterparts. The Steering Committee meets on a near bimonthly basis to discuss topics drawn from a pre-circulated agenda. Subcommittees are formed on an ad-hoc basis to address specific topics of interest to the members.

EVALUATION

The JLMC monitors all industry contracts about to expire and offers to mediate settlements in key collective bargaining situations. It has helped bring about peaceful settlements in five of eight disputes covering about 82,000 bargaining unit workers.

The JLMC has used its subcommittees to address specific work issues and has achieved some positive results. Regulations affecting retail meat cutters formulated by JLMC, for example, were adopted in their entirety by OSHA, as were recommendations resulting from a five-year JLMC-initiated study by the Harvard School of Public Health on the possible effects of materials and working conditions in retail meat departments. New policies stemming from the impact of Universal Product Code (UPC) technology were also developed.

The JLMC has published two studies on methods of containing health care cost increases, both of which have been widely circulated: ''Putting a Lid on Health Care Costs'' (1980) and ''A Joint Labor Management Communication on Health Care Cost Management'' (1985). Other JLMC research has involved productivity measurement, unfunded liability of multi-employer pension funds and health and welfare plans, multi-tier wage settlements, alcohol and substance abuse, and data collection within the industry.

The work conducted by the JLMC has even greater significance now that sales in the retail foods industry has exceeded ten percent of this country's gross national product, and employment has reached nearly 3 million workers. It has proved over a long period of time (1974–1987) that ''working together'' can provide benefits that ''working as adversaries'' cannot.

Contact: Nicholas A. Fidandis
Chairman
Joint Labor Management Committee
  of the Retail Food Industry
2120 L Street, N.W., Suite 245
Washington, D.C. 20037
(202) 331–0950

It isn't easy to change. It's easier to do things the way you've always done them. It's easier to concentrate on "things" than to try to understand and develop people. But in a competitive, rapidly changing marketplace, doing things the same old way just won't do. We need to be creative, innovative, and energetic.

—Vern Lindstrom
President

KITCHELL CORPORATION

Comprehensive Participative Management Program Helps to Develop New Managers for Future Growth

THE PROGRAM

Like many of today's top executives, President Vern Lindstrom of the Kitchell Corporation wanted to find a way to institutionalize the entrepreneurial spirit that had helped his company grow well beyond the small family firm that could communicate easily within one office. He felt that the need to develop a new kind of manager, in particular, was critical for the success of this company's future expansion plans.

Lindstrom's solution was the People Management System, a plan he says will help Kitchell "to produce and communicate in a more efficient manner, provide proper performance evaluation and recognition, and have more employee participation in the management of the company." The system has already been integrated into the strategic plans for the company and includes a number of important components:
- an organizational structure designed for flexibility and growth
- personnel planning to meet future needs
- a performance evaluation system
- an employee relations plan to meet employee needs for direction and recognition
- a company-wide productivity plan
- a progressive compensation, incentive, and reward system
- a personnel administration system to monitor working conditions
- an employee communications plan
- a comprehensive marketing and sales system

• a computer integration plan.

At first, Lindstrom had to hire a number of communications, education, and productivity directors to develop and coordinate all these programs. Using technical, political, and cultural change models, a flexible organizational structure for continued growth was implemented. Then employee communications were expanded and task forces developed to generate involvement and input and new computer technology was integrated into the company.

A performance evaluation system was set up that reinforces one-to-one relationships between employees and supervisors, and sets goals and performance standards that are reviewed quarterly. The system is also designed to identify areas where further training and education is needed—in an effort to develop the kind of management strength and depth that will be needed in the future.

Kitchell also utilizes a consultant to implement a program that it says will help the company's employees become more effective as individuals and as a team. Called Educational Development for Growth and Effectiveness, or EDGE, the program has been made available to all employees on a voluntary basis, as well as to their spouses and high-school-age children. The first part of the program, Increasing Human Effectiveness, provides concepts, techniques, and skills necessary to prepare for a climate of active teamwork and cooperation. In order to promote consistently high performance and job satisfaction, a common language for goal setting and problem solving is also developed.

The second part of the program concentrates on team building and is specifically designed for the senior management group of each Kitchell company and for managers within individual departments. Here, teams of managers work to develop a mission statement with shared values and to establish a set of goals to add consistency to long-range planning. By having managers identify personal, departmental, and company values, and engage in trust-building exercises, the program helps them develop self-esteem and mutual respect within their groups.

The third and final aspect of the program is plan maintenance, which consists of periodic visits by consultants to monitor the effectiveness of the program, assist individuals who are having implementation problems, and strengthen the team-building process where needed.

EVALUATION

Although the Kitchell Corporation has not attempted formally to measure the results of its program, the company has improved its capture ratio for marketing, increased its sales volume, achieved higher profit margins, lowered turnover, and earned recognition within its industry, all since implementing various components of the People Management System. Employee feedback on the benefits of the program has been consistently positive, and overall employee morale has improved significantly.

Though it has been restricted by limited human and financial resources, and has had to be phased in slowly over a four-year period, the People Management System has prompted a great deal of effort to restructure the company and to create a receptivity to change and willingness to innovate. Employee input so far has resulted in a number of significant systems improvements and some promising new concepts for improving productivity.

Contact: Barbara Bean
Director of Communications
Kitchell Corporation
1006 South 24th Street
Phoenix, Arizona 85034
(602) 275-7541

> Workers should be paid on the basis of their
> accomplishments and efficiencies; they should
> share in the profits their efforts make possible.
> —James F. Lincoln
> Founder

LINCOLN ELECTRIC COMPANY

Incentive System Helps Maximize Both Wages and Profits for
Welding Equipment Manufacturer

THE PROGRAM

The statement above, made by James F. Lincoln in 1952, still holds true at
Lincoln Electric today. Workers are paid more when they help bring about work
efficiencies, and they share in the profits of the company.

To accomplish the former, Lincoln attempts to operate as many jobs as possible on a straight piecework basis. Piece standards are permanently fixed and
change only if a different method, material, or machine is introduced in any
particular operation. Any worker who can figure out a way to produce above
standard receives more pay and Lincoln does not limit the amount of money an
employee can earn.

Employees are given a share of the company's profits through a bonus paid in a
lump sum at the end of the fiscal year. (The company feels it is not possible to
determine success on a shorter basis and still be fair to both shareholders and
employees.) After a dividend is declared and the future cash needs of the company are taken care of, the balance is distributed among all employees at a rate,
expressed as a percentage of base pay, that is determined by the board of directors.

Bonus Example

Annual Wage Rate	Company % Bonus Rate	Merit Rating of Employee %	Computed Bonus	Total Compensation
$17,000	100%	85	$14,450	$31,450
$24,000	100%	118	$28,320	$52,320

All employees are reviewed for merit ratings twice each year, and in this process, each employee is compared to other members of his or her merit rating group. Everyone is evaluated in four categories: ideas and cooperation, output, dependability, and quality. Merit ratings range between 80 and 120 percent.

Lincoln Electric feels that a compensation system that combines piecework with bonuses creates a strong motivating factor at both the individual and group levels. Employees feel they are competing with themselves, not their peers and everyone knows that he or she has the same chance and opportunity to excel.

The system also encourages cooperation, because bonuses are tied directly to company profits. Peer pressure and individual feelings of accountability help ensure that everyone does his or her part. According to Harry Carlson, a company executive, "employees want to increase both the total pool and their cut of that pool."

Managers also play an an important role in enhancing the system by working to break down any and all barriers that may hinder individual performance. "Managers must allow latent abilities to come to the surface," says Carlson. "The whole idea is to give people the opportunity to do a better job today than they did yesterday."

EVALUATION

At Lincoln Electric, employees are considered valuable assets and, as such, they are treated honestly, respectfully, and generously. The average bonus paid out in 1986 was $16,000. That year, some production employees earned over $60,000, and factory workers' total earnings were better yet in 1987. The company imposes no mandatory retirement age, and guarantees all employees at least 30 hours of work each week. Even in the 1982 recession, no one was laid off.

Today, many companies embrace the slogan, "Work smarter, not harder." But given the work ethic he helped develop in his own company, James Lincoln would probably have preferred the slogan, "Work smarter and harder."

Contact: Richard S. Sabo
Assistant to CEO
The Lincoln Electric Company
22801 St. Clair Avenue
Cleveland, Ohio 44117
(216) 481–8100

*Why an employee stock ownership plan? It's the
most dynamic, the most flexible employee
gainsharing plan I know of.*

—Robert Strickland
Chairman

LOWE'S COMPANIES, INC.

Employees in Specialty Retail Chain Work for Themselves Through Employee Stock Ownership Plan

THE PROGRAM

Motivating employees by giving them a stake in their company is not a new technique. For years, employee stock ownership plans (ESOPs) have been used as effective vehicles for sharing financial benefits among all those who contribute to bringing them about. One of the oldest and most successful ESOPs in the country is the one at Lowe's Companies, Inc.

Lowe's ESOP story is a truly dynamic one. In 1975, *Newsweek* featured an article describing a Lowe's employee who had never earned more than $125 a week but who retired with $660,000 in Lowe's stock. Like all Lowe's employees, he did not have to contribute a penny of his personal funds to buy the stock, because each year the company puts aside up to 15 percent of its payroll to be invested in its ESOP plan.

Lowe's Chairman Robert Strickland is the program's most enthusiastic spokesperson. He will tell anyone that, without a doubt, the company's ESOP plan has been a key ingredient of its success.

> How do I know it works? How do I know that Lowe's growth wasn't influenced more by geography, or the business we're in, or management skill? Because in the late 1950s and early 1960s, there were at least five other companies just like ours in the Sunbelt: one in Virginia, one in South Carolina, one in Florida, and two in North Carolina. The same geography, the same business—different management, of course, but not bad management. Three of the companies didn't make it on their own and sold out. The fourth company is about one-fourth our

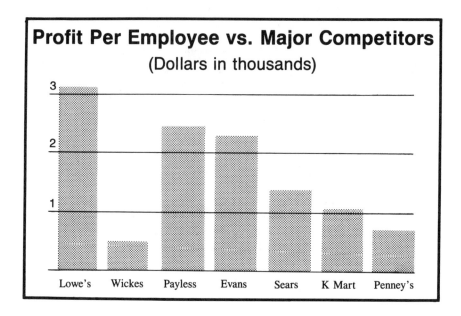

size and has just adopted an employee stock ownership plan. It was a case of survival of the most motivated and the most productive.

One question many people ask about ESOPs is, what happens to employee motivation when the price of the company stock drops? According to Personnel Director Ed Spears, no one at Lowe's seems to mind. Employees there are sophisticated enough to understand that the conditions that cause stock prices to fluctuate are usually temporary. Some even look forward to an occasional price drop because they realize that the company can then purchase more stock than it could at a higher price. The October 1987 stock market crash, for instance, gave employees just such an opportunity and they took advantage of it.

The ESOP plan at Lowe's is now an integral part of the company's identity. Employees like it because it provides them with a substantial financial package for their retirement, and management likes it because it helps keep the work force highly motivated and productive.

EVALUATION

Lowe's ESOP program has been such a continuing success that at the end of 1986 the company released the following statement:

> We are extremely proud of our ESOP, which has proven to be an outstanding asset for our company, our employee shareholders, and our other shareholders as

well. All employees completing 1,000 hours of service and one full year of employment are eligible for membership. They have full voting rights on all shares allocated to their accounts on an annual basis. In 1986 we were able to pass through to employee shareholders cash dividends totaling $2.1 million. These funds were deducted from our federal taxable income, resulting in a tax benefit of $1.1 million, which was treated as an addition to capital surplus. This year's funding of $11.6 million of our ESOP contribution with 300,000 shares of new stock, raised new equity capital in the most cost-effective way. The ESOP trust is Lowe's largest shareholder, with approximately 18 percent ownership of the company.

Contact: Ed Spears
Director of Personnel
Lowe's Companies, Inc.
P.O. Box 1111
North Wilkesboro, North Carolina 28656
(919) 651–4000

The payroll savings helped us through a tough time for the company, and kept everyone in a job.

—Linda Steel
Personnel Director

McCREARY TIRE & RUBBER COMPANY

Distributing Layoffs through Furlough Rotation Helps Tire Manufacturer Cut Direct Labor Costs and Shift into New Lines of Production

THE PROGRAM

Like a lot of other companies trying to weather the recession of 1982, McCreary Tire and Rubber Company was losing money—the recession had dramatically reduced demand for its passenger tires. As part of a long-range plan to cut costs and shift to manufacturing truck and specialty tires, the company decided to implement a rotating furlough system instead of laying off a large portion of its work force.

Each week, one third of the company's 400 production workers were "laid off" on a rotating basis. Each employee would work for two weeks and then, under an agreement with the State of Pennsylvania, collect supplemental payments for less than full-time employment during the third week, when the employee would be on furlough. In this way, every McCreary employee was able to work two of every three weeks through the summer of 1982, as the troubled company shifted into a more profitable production line.

EVALUATION

Even though the rotating furlough system has the effect of increasing a company's future payroll taxes, it did save jobs for workers at McCreary and helped the company survive the 1982 recession. In addition, productivity rose, absenteeism fell, on-the-job injuries decreased, and employee relations improved, at least in the short term.

The McCreary study ends on a less positive note, however. In March of 1983 the company union went out on strike for about six weeks, and the furlough program was shelved. As the Pennsylvania economy improved during the next few years, job security was increased and employees forgot about the problems they had experienced during the summer of 1982.

But in March of 1986 the company union went out on strike again, and McCreary replaced all its unionized employees with non-union workers or new hires. This dispute was never settled and a decertification election was held by the National Labor Relations Board in March 1988, when McCreary's employees voted 181 to 5 against joining the union.

Today, McCreary says it still believes in the rotating furlough system and would certainly reinstate it should the Pennsylvania economy experience another recession. It was a good idea, the company reminds us, but like all such plans, it is not a panacea.

Contact: Linda Steel
Personnel Director
McCreary Tire & Rubber Company
P.O. Box 749
Indiana, Pennsylvania 15701–0749
(412) 349–9010

*Motorola has evolved to its present state by a
determination to manage our physical,
financial, and human resources more effectively
and efficiently than before.*

—Ralph Ponce DeLeon
Manager

MOTOROLA, INC.

Electronics Manufacturer Initiates Participative Management
Program that Gives Everyone a Chance to Improve the Business

THE PROGRAM

Motorola, a company of over 90,000 employees, has always sought to remain as
decentralized as possible while still maintaining the financial welfare of the entire
organization. Every profit center is run as if it were a separate company, each
with its own engineering and marketing departments, all in an effort to retain a
small-company, entrepreneurial, proprietary atmosphere.

At Motorola, the determination to improve its competitive position and its
productivity took the form of a companywide effort called the Participative
Management Program (PMP), and PMP is a natural extension of company's
policy of decentralization. It works by breaking down each operating unit into
logical teams whose sole purpose is to make every employee a key contributor to
serving the customer better, and thus improving the success of the business.
Under the rules of PMP, each team is given a set of performance goals, and if
these goals are met and the company meets its overall return on net assets target, a
bonus is paid to each team member.

Any employees who are not commissioned salespeople or participants in the
Executive Incentive Program can take part in PMP. The goals for PMP are set by
a steering committee, which bases its decisions on both strategic operating and
human resource considerations, such as: (1) quality, (2) current costs, (3) delivery, (4) inventory, (5) housekeeping and safety, and (6) cost reduction. All goals
are quantified so that they can be easily measured on a regular basis, and every
team conducts a monthly session to determine how well it is doing in meeting
them.

Bonuses are distributed when a team meets its own goals, the profit center it
belongs to achieves the pre-tax profit it had planned and the entire company meets

its overall profit target. (The company added the overall company profitability requirement in 1988 to make sure that decentralization does not lead to destructive internal competition.) When all three conditions are met, a portion of the profit earned is made available for bonuses, with the amount paid to each participant determined by that person's share of the team's total payroll.

As with most productivity programs, management's role has been key to the success of PMP, and at Motorola, its most important job has been to create the kind of environment and atmosphere in which every person can contribute the most of what he or she has to offer. The backing and blessing of top management has also helped. In a recent speech, Vice Chairman and Chief Operating Officer William J. Weisz told his audience that PMP is now and will continue to be one of the most important contributors to Motorola's success.

> We believe that participative management, together with our fundamental policy of continuous decentralization, will make it possible to lead and work our behemoth successfully and artfully in the 80's and beyond. PMP is a counterbalancing force to size, breaking challenges down to where individual employees can see the results of their participation.

Training has also been a strongly emphasized aspect of the program. And Motorola's philosophy is to provide the kind of training that encourages employees to understand the relationship between quality, productivity, and customer service, and to instill in them a basic understanding of "what our customers mean." This type of training is essential for the program to succeed, says management, because everyone's job is interrelated to everyone else's and it is important that all Motorola employees learn to think as a team.

EVALUATION

Since PMP was initiated in 1968, Motorola's employees have had a strong voice in how their company is run, and that has helped keep morale and product quality at a high level. The company also believes that PMP has helped it "to provide the customer with the best possible product and service, in compliance with the customer's delivery schedule, at the lowest possible cost."

Although it is against company policy to release specific financial figures, Motorola says that PMP continues to bring about widespread cost savings, along with improvements in employee health and safety, and has helped the company successfully weather the economic turbulence of the 1980s.

Contact: Julie Sackett
VP and Director of Personnel
Government Electronics Group
Motorola, Inc.
P.O. Box 1417
Scottsdale, Arizona 85252

I went through two Toyota assembly plants and a stamping plant in Japan and they have a fast pace. But their system is laid out so that it's easier for the worker to do the job than it is here.

—Bruce Lee
Manager

NEW UNITED MOTOR MANUFACTURING INC.

UAW Joins Japanese Management in Manufacturing Small Cars in California; Will It Work?

THE PROGRAM

When Japanese imports began to account for a sizable share of the huge California automobile market, the General Motors Corporation and Toyota decided to work together to produce both Japanese and American cars in the U.S. Together they converted a former GM assembly plant in Fremont, California, into a new company that would produce 650 Chevy Novas and Toyota Corollas a day using only unionized labor. Today 85 percent of the plant's former workers hold jobs in this new company called New United Motor Manufacturing Inc. (NUMMI).

If NUMMI can succeed in producing cars to Japan's high-quality standards and with a unionized American work force, the venture could force profound changes throughout the U.S. auto industry. NUMMI has agreed to hire only furloughed workers from UAW's Local 1364 (now Local 2244) and has agreed to a no-layoff policy unless the fundamental, long-term viability of the company is jeopardized. In return, the UAW has agreed to accept NUMMI as a new venture not bound by seniority rights, work rules, or rigid job classifications. A Japanese-style management system has been put in place.

All assembly workers at NUMMI have a single job classification and are organized into work teams of five to seven people, each of whom is cross-trained in all team jobs. Skilled trades people are divided into only three classifications— tool and die, tool and die tryout, and maintenance—and all maintenance personnel are trained to work in all skill areas (electricity, metal plumbing, etc.)

The organizational hierarchy within the company consists of just six layers:

1. team members,

2. leaders of teams with four to six members (non-supervisory),
3. group leaders with three teams,
4. assistant managers,
5. managers, and
6. executive officers (vice-president for engineering, vice-president for quality control, vice-president for manufacturing, and president).

Management responsibility lies primarily with the teams, and only five layers of Japanese and American managers supervise the entire plant—one or two layers less than the typical U.S. plant—and with fewer managers at each level.

Since U.S. workers are used to receiving higher wages than their Japanese counterparts, NUMMI has worked to keep its labor costs down by adopting HMO health care and a nontraditional defined-contribution pension plan.

EVALUATION

Production at NUMMI began in December 1984, and its performance standards were set for higher quality and lower cost. So far, results in both areas have exceeded the company's original expectations.

Today, NUMMI-produced cars are widely recognized as high-quality vehicles. They are repeatedly ranked well above average by independent automotive magazines, and in numerous surveys the Nova has come out number one in production quality among all American-made cars.

In addition, the quality of cooperation between management and labor at NUMMI now serves as a model not only for the auto industry, but for U.S. business in general.

Contact: Thomas Klipstone
Manager of Community Relations
NUMMI (New United Motor Manufacturing Inc.)
45500 Fremont Boulevard
Fremont, California 94538
(415) 498-5666

Stan Jones
International Representative
UAW Local 2244
45201 Fremont Boulevard
Fremont, California 94538
(415) 656-9901

The BME's experience belies the common notions that government workers cannot be as productive as their private-sector counterparts or that the output of a governmental operation cannot be measured. There is no simple formula for succeeding in the change from a traditional approach to the labor/management approach. It must begin with a critical factor—management's commitment to share its power with labor and some degree of imagination in devising accurate, but nonthreatening, ways to measure productivity. But given the effort and the true desire to see it succeed, it does work.

—Ron Contino
Deputy Commissioner

NYC DEPARTMENT OF SANITATION

Employee Participation Program Transforms New York City Bureau Into ''Profit Center''

THE PROGRAM

When Ron Contino was appointed deputy commissioner for Support Operations in 1978, the Bureau of Motor Equipment (BME) in New York City's Department of Sanitation was widely regarded as being in a state of total chaos. Responsible for the largest municipal fleet of vehicles in the country, the BME had 1,200 employees, seven major central repair facilities, and seventy-three satellite repair garages throughout the five boroughs. Almost half its sanitation trucks were unavailable on any given day, overtime was excessive and growing, and substantial rework was all too common.

Contino turned the BME around by using a two-part program of reform. After winning top management support, he organized permanent, full-time union/management committees to address the problems employees were having in performing their work. Then he abolished individual work standards and bean to measure output only at the whole shop level. This, he believed, would help ensure that no employee labored at tasks that were unproductive and would provide the kind of peer pressure that would help the BME operate at the same level of efficiency as the private sector.

The Management Information System Contino had installed to monitor the progress of the program was also truly unique. It allows the bureau to calculate the costs of the various activities it performs and to compare those costs to the prices charged for the same services by vendors in the private sector. If repairing a transmission, for example, costs less for the bureau to do itself than to purchase, it will be retained as a job within the BME. But if it is determined that the service can be performed more cheaply by an outside vendor, the BME will shift its efforts to other work areas where it can be more productive. This aspect of the program was modified in 1986 to allow other city departments to submit bids for BME jobs—such as the fire department for emergency services. The newest program is a joint venture with the private sector to develop a new type of tire for New York's municipal fleet. Any savings that accumulate from the venture will be returned to the civil service work force through improvements in the quality of their work environment.

EVALUATION

By turning the BME into a "profit center" and by prominently displaying its productivity gains, Contino has helped focus everyone's efforts toward achieving the kind of results that will be felt citywide.

One of BME's components is a landfill operation; suggestions for this alone have resulted in a realized annual cost avoidance of $114,000 and a projected annual cost avoidance of $155,000. These included design modifications to equipment needed to reduce downtime and plans to save money by manufacturing in-house expensive repair parts that would normally be purchased from outside vendors.

Overall, the eight shops involved in Contino's program are operating at a "profit center" productivity of 1.41, which means that every dollar invested in them by the city is producing goods and services that would cost $1.41 if purchased from the private sector. In 1986, that translated into an annual "profit" for the BME of $3.9 million.

Contact: Ronald Contino
Deputy Commissioner
Support Operations
Bureau of Motor Equipment
New York City Department of Sanitation
Room 819
125 Worth Street
New York, New York 10013
(212) 566-5247

Those managements which require rigid patterns
of conformance are depriving the company of
new ideas, better ideas, and innovations.
—F. Kenneth Iverson
Chairman and CEO

NUCOR CORPORATION

New Steel Technology Results in Lower Manufacturing Costs

THE PROGRAM

In 1970, most U.S. steel manufacturers relied on the costly ingot processing method to make their steel products. First, hot metal had to be poured into ingots, then it was reheated and rolled into billets for shaping. Time-consuming and resource-intensive, this process could take up to two weeks to complete. To achieve a competitive edge, Nucor decided to use a new technology based on continuous casting.

In the continuous casting process, selected scrap iron and alloy elements are melted together and then poured into a continuous casting billet system. The high pre-heat temperature in the ladle and a sliding gate valve permit a constant flow of liquid steel that is directly converted into billets, thereby eliminating all the cooling, reheating, and rolling that was once required with ingots.

Quality control at Nucor is also an important factor throughout the continuous casting process. Samples are tested for chemical ratios, yield, tensile strengths, and elongation, and a computer is used to determine whether the tested materials conform to standard.

EVALUATION

Nucor remains one of the most profitable steel firms in America, and the continuous casting process is the principal reason for its success. It has increased the company's capacity, reduced its material and energy costs, and substantially lowered the prices the company must charge customers for its finished products.

The ongoing search for new manufacturing methods has kept Nucor up-to-date and competitive with companies around the world.

Contact: F. Kenneth Iverson
Chairman and Chief Executive Officer
Nucor Corporation
4425 Randolph Road
Charlotte, North Carolina 28211
(704) 366-7000

The real art of management lies in the maximum utilization of ordinary men and women. Since these are always in plentiful supply, long-term success will go to those who know how to release the energy, zest, and hidden potential in us all.

—John G. Quay
Training and Development Specialist

PALATINE POLICE DEPARTMENT

Dual Career Ladder Offers Police Officers Higher Earnings for Expanded Competence and Increases Departmental Productivity

THE PROGRAM

Bringing out the "hidden potential" in employees can be a difficult task. But the police department in Palatine, Illinois, has been able to do it through an innovative career advancement program called Dual Career Ladder (DCL).

The DCL was developed because the traditional career ladder that existed for police officers in Palatine was failing to address many of their frustrations and concerns. Though many officers were motivated by the promise of advancement, the structure of the department actually restricted such upward movement and provided few promotional opportunities. Nor did the system recognize and reward officers whose performance was superior to that of their peers or identify those officers whose performance was below standard. Finally, the system clearly lacked career alternatives for police officers who wanted to make more money but still wanted to remain "on the street."

After three years discussing the merits and possible effectiveness of the DCL, the Board of Trustees formally committed itself to the program and presentations were made to all department personnel. A task force was assigned to transform the concept into a working program and five subcommittees were established to examine specific topics; any police officer who was interested in a topic could become a member of the subcommittee that dealt with it.

The DCL works essentially by expanding the concept of lateral mobility. Any officer can make a lateral move as long as he or she meets several program requirements. These include: (1) at least one year at the top of his or her current pay classification, (2) proficiency in twenty-five knowledge and skill areas,

(3) proficiency in a number of advanced skill and knowledge areas (the number depending on the pay level desired), (4) continuing education course work (the amount depending on the hiring date of the officer), and (5) satisfactory maintenance of overall job performance standards (measured by the number of tickets written, the number of criminal arrests made, etc.).

Each lateral "advancement" includes a pay bonus, identifiable insignia, recognition by the department, and increased job responsibility. After a year in the new job, the officer is required to pass through the selection process again in order to retain his or her position or advance to a new one.

EVALUATION

Developed without the assistance of any federal dollars, the DCL has been able to increase productivity at the Palatine Police Department by almost 10 percent. Over the years, it has been modified and other programs have been added, but it still remains a vital mechanism for maintaining morale and ensuring top-flight performance.

Though they were developed solely by and for the use of the Palatine Police Department, the concepts and structures of the Dual Career Ladder program may prove useful in many nongovernmental organizations that are also dealing with the problems created by traditional—and perhaps antiquated—career advancement systems.

Contact: Walter D. Gasior
Deputy Chief, Support Services Division
Palatine Police Department
200 East Wood Street
Palatine, Illinois 60067–5332
(312) 358–7102

Many evaluations cite benefits for which a monetary value cannot be given.
—PENNTAP 1986 "Update"

PENNTAP

Costly Technical Assistance and Information Available to Businesses Free

THE PROGRAM

In 1965, the state of Pennsylvania decided to help its 200,000 small businesses acquire the technical, scientific, and engineering know-how they would need in order to prosper and remain competitive. So a partnership was established between Pennsylvania State University and the state Department of Commerce to provide a free service called PENNTAP.

PENNTAP may be used by any business owner, operator, or representative in Pennsylvania who has a problem simply by contacting the main office in University Park or any one of the twenty-seven other commonwealth offices. One of PENNTAP's part-time specialists will be assigned to the problem and may assist the user by offering suggestions based on personal experience, consultations with other PENNTAP specialists or Penn State faculty members, library or computer research, or an investigation into federal resources. When all the information on the problem is assembled, it is usually presented to the user in the form of several possible solutions, and always in understandable terms.

For their part, users are asked only to complete an evaluation form at some time in the future when the results of their contact with PENNTAP can be measured.

EVALUATION

So far, PENNTAP has provided $102 million worth of economic assistance to Pennsylvania's economy for only $6 million—a cost-benefit ratio of 17.9 to 1.

Though few business people are aware of it, the U.S. government will also provide businesses with direct access to virtually every aspect of unclassified government research—free of charge, simply by contacting the U.S. government's federal laboratories. Specific referrals can be made by the U.S. Office of Science and Technology Policy, Washington D.C., 20506, telephone (202) 395-3000.

Contact: Dr. H. LeRoy Marlow
Director
Pennsylvania Technical Assistance Program
Pennsylvania State University
501 Keller Building
University Park, Pennsylvania 16802
(814) 865-0427

Our organization has set a course for productivity growth which is based on quality products and our people's desire to perform.
—*Bruce Los*
Development Manager

PRINCE CORPORATION

Pay-for-Performance Program Helps Auto Parts Manufacturer
Evaluate Employees More Objectively

THE PROGRAM

The Prince Corporation wanted to establish a more direct correlation between the productivity of its workers and their pay. So the company developed a sophisticated pay-for-performance program that evaluates each employee's work performance in five different areas: (1) attendance, (2) quality, (3) quantity, (4) cooperation, and (5) work rules. Each Prince employee receives a numerical score for each of the five areas, and the employee's hourly wage is directly tied to the total score achieved. Work performance reviews are conducted on a quarterly basis for the first three years of employment with the company and on an annual basis every year thereafter.

What happens when an employee's score drops? He or she is given another three months to bring the score to its previous level, but if it does not return, the employee's hourly pay rate is adjusted downward. Prince's philosophy is that everyone should be held accountable for his or her own actions—and rewarded accordingly—and the program has become such an integral part of the company's overall operations that President John Spoelhof reviews evaluations periodically to make sure the evaluators are doing their job.

Grading employees in the areas of attendance, quantity, and adherence to work rules is relatively easy but it may be a lot trickier for a supervisor to evaluate an employee's quality and cooperation. So all employees at Prince are expected to audit the quality of their own work using an objective rating system, and to post the results daily. This evaluation technique produces two important benefits for the company: it confirms management's belief in the integrity of each employee, and it provides each employee with immediate feedback on those areas that need improvement.

Another important part of Prince's pay-for-performance program is its bonus system. Distributed once a year, bonuses are based on: (1) the corporation's overall profitability, (2) each division's profitability, and (3) each employee's work performance. Such a system, says Spoelhof, allows employees to feel that they work for themselves *and* that they are part of a team, which helps "build responsibility within themselves, their division, and the corporation."

EVALUATION

Prince measures the success of its pay-for-performance system in terms of customer satisfaction. The company has received top-notch ratings from each of the major automakers it serves and that has helped it enjoy remarkably steady growth. In addition, pay-for-performance fits very well within the company's overall corporate philosophy: "mutual trust and respect."

Contact: Bruce Los
Development Manager
Prince Corporation
1 Prince Center
Holland, Michigan 49423
(616) 392–5151

We decided to pay people a weekly salary with the amount determined by the number of different jobs an individual could perform. There would be no time clocks or watchmen.

—Stan Holditch
Retired Plant Manager

THE PROCTER & GAMBLE COMPANY

Job Enlargement Plan Based on Pay-for-Skills and Delegation of Responsibility Creates P&G's Most Productive Plant

BACKGROUND

The Procter & Gamble Company (P&G) has a long history of innovative employee recognition programs: profit sharing was introduced in 1887, a Guaranteed Employment Plan was adopted in 1923, and a comprehensive employee benefits program was instituted in 1930. P&G's pay levels were high and its vacation benefits were generous, yet the company was not satisfied with the general levels of employee relations, motivation, and productivity.

What management sensed as an undercurrent of disgruntlement was being reflected in conflicts with workers over the administration of incentive pay and the standards used to determine compensation. New technology was being resisted with slowdowns and grievances, and productivity was declining and costs rising because many operations were trying to beat the "incentive system."

Recognizing the need to resolve these problems before they caused further damage to the company, its employees, and its customers, P&G assembled a task force of managers and experts drawn from all areas of the company and charged it with the responsibility of coming up with some solutions. The general conclusions reached by this task force were that P&G's employees would perform better if their job assignments included:

1. greater responsibility for making decisions and for taking actions that affect their personal future,

2. more diverse tasks of sufficient scope to provide greater challenges and a sense of accomplishment,

3. more accountability for planning and executing their work assignments and for evaluating their work once it is completed,

4. the opportunity to learn new skills and to experience personal growth on the job, and

5. recognition from their peers and superiors for playing an important part in meeting company goals and in setting personal performance standards.

THE PROGRAM

To test the conclusions reached by the task force, the decision was made to apply these new concepts in a completely new plant, being planned for Lima, Ohio, that would make consumer household products. The concepts were applied in the following ways:

1. The plant was organized into production teams, each responsible for operating a major part of the plant on its shift.

2. Each production team was comprised of process technicians, packing technicians, and warehouse technicians, who together were responsible for the product from raw materials to final shipment and accounting.

3. Production team members were salaried personnel, and salary levels were determined by the number of different jobs an individual could perform.

4. The number of managerial positions in the plant was reduced to only one-fifth those in a comparable P&G manufacturing facility. No time clocks or production overseers were used.

5. Clerical, laboratory, and other specialist positions were eliminated, while maintenance and clean-up jobs were contracted out.

6. Equipment was designed according to specific process needs and mainte-nance saving features were added whenever possible.

EVALUATION

The Lima, Ohio, plant started operations in 1967 and quickly became a model for other new or converting P&G plants. Although start-up was challenging both for the plant's workers and for corporate management, the Lima facility achieved its projected targets within only one year. By the end of the first year, in fact, it was:

• first in production volume of any plant in the company, filling as many as seventy-five railroad cars a day with the output of fewer than 200 people;

• first in quality production within the company;

• operating at lower costs than comparable plants within the company (and after four years operating at 40 percent of the cost of other P&G plants);

• able to remain in operation during a two-day blizzard that paralyzed produc-tion at other midwestern plants;

• successful in modifying its packing lines to permit the use of new bottles (designed by a plant technician, not an engineer or manager, who in six months organized and implemented the changes required);

• able to solve numerous problems arising from the purchase of bottles not uniform in size nor according to specification, with the visit of a plant technician to the bottle manufacturer (where her meetings with management and machine operators resulted in a marked improvement in bottle quality).

Although this job enlargement approach to motivating employees works in old facilities as well as new ones, P&G's experience indicates that newer production environments, with more modern layouts, and more advanced equipment, and a new work force, can contribute to producing quicker and more certain results.

Contact: Stan Holditch
Procter & Gamble Lima Plant Manager (Retired)
28295 Via Rueda
San Juan Capistrano, California 28295
(714) 661-8697

If we were going to keep the AFL-CIO alive, we
had to keep the AFL-CIO contractors in
business. You just begin by taking the first step.
—Richard Mantia
AFL-CIO Executive

PRODUCTIVITY AND RESPONSIBILITY INCREASE DEVELOPMENT AND EMPLOYMENT (PRIDE)

Construction Industry Cooperation Succeeds in St. Louis, Leads to Similar Efforts Across the U.S.

THE PROGRAM

Back in 1972, St. Louis had a notorious reputation as a difficult trade union city. Jurisdictional strikes were closing construction sites several times a month, local businesses were delaying expansion because of the tensions, the number of labor hours worked was falling, and open shops were gaining contracts. Both union and construction leaders realized that unless serious changes were made, neither of them was going to survive.

It was then that leaders of the Building and Construction Trades Council decided to sit down with the Associated General Contractors in an attempt to improve the city's construction climate. Together with the input of architects, engineers, and material suppliers, they drew up a "memorandum of understanding" called PRIDE—Productivity and Responsibility Increase Development and Employment. Based on the concept of compromise, its goals were to increase construction productivity, development, and employment within the St. Louis area. Union work rules were eased, featherbedding was eliminated, jurisdictional strikes were banned, and on-site management control was strengthened. Non-binding arbitration through PRIDE was established in return for a no-picket-line pledge during contract strikes, and city contractors agreed to employ only union labor.

Perhaps the most important achievement of PRIDE, however, was preventa-

175

tive. In an attempt to improve productivity, and to resolve burgeoning problems before they became serious, monthly meetings of PRIDE were set up to evaluate the status of the construction industry in St. Louis on a continuing basis.

EVALUATION

Even though PRIDE had no paid staff (two-thirds of its $7,000 budget was funded by contractors and one-third by its union members), it worked! Construction in the St. Louis area was rejuvenated—overall productivity rose between 10 and 15 percent—and trade union membership reached full employment. Within a short time, 98 percent of the city's commercial and industrial construction and 96 percent of its residential construction were being built with AFL-CIO labor. Projects were being completed in time and under budget, and all parties were benefiting from this cooperative effort at boosting productivity.

The success of PRIDE in St. Louis has already spawned at least ten similar programs around the country. These include MOST (Management and Organized Labor Striving Together) in Columbus, Ohio; PEP (Planning Economic Progress) in Beaumont, Texas; UNION JACK in Denver, Colorado; and TOP NOTCH in Indianapolis, Indiana.

Contact:
Building and Construction Trades
    Council of St. Louis
2300 Hampton Street
St. Louis, Missouri 63139
(314) 647–0628

*The Company should be organized and conduct
its affairs in such a manner as to make, as
nearly as possible, each individual's work
situation akin to what it would be if he or she
were working for himself or herself.*
—*John May
Director of Education and Training*

THE PRUDENTIAL INSURANCE COMPANY OF AMERICA

Job Redesign Increases Employee Motivation and Results in
53 Percent Quality Improvement

THE PROGRAM

It was sometime during the 1960s when The Prudential Insurance Company
realized that the proliferation of poorly designed clerical jobs within the company
was frustrating its attempts to attract and retain high-quality employees. To
combat this situation, the president announced his intention to develop the kind of
"work environment that should encourage every Prudential man and woman to
work creatively."

As a start, the company administered a lengthy employee survey to measure
job attitudes and pinpoint areas where job design would do the most good. Then,
an experimental effort was initiated in the ten home offices, the early results of
which indicated that it would be advisable to implement the program companywide. The program had three main objectives:

1. to improve productivity, reduce error rates, and improve service,
2. to raise the level of job satisfaction on a long-term basis, and
3. to make job design an integral part of management strategy.

To ensure the success of the program, The Prudential developed a seven-point
implementation strategy that included:

1. establishing regional and home office task force teams,
2. training and developing job design consultants,
3. publishing a 400-page "how to" manual for the consultants as a training
tool and reference guide,
4. appointing a job design consultant to each Prudential office,

5. conducting workshops for all those who would be involved in job redesign in their areas,

6. conducting special training workshops for computer programmers in each office,

7. creating a training session for The Prudential auditing staff on job design concepts.

EVALUATION

In 1984, the consolidation of work brought about by The Prudential's job redesign effort made it possible for the company to reduce the number of its regional offices from eight to four. In addition, the program is credited with raising service levels 60 percent, improving quality by 53 percent, and boosting morale 61 percent. More than 90 percent of the company's managers felt that the job redesign effort has met or exceeded their original expectations of it.

Today, job redesign at The Prudential is no longer considered a special "program." It has become an integral part of the company's way of life, and all new jobs are designed with the needs of the employees in mind. What is more, the motivation behind this effort to design more satisfying and more creative jobs has spread to other areas of the company and has resulted in the development of quality circles, productivity improvement groups, organizational climate assessment techniques, career development efforts, and new training programs for performance appraisal systems.

Contact: Joan Ellen
Human Resources
The Prudential Insurance Company of America
745 Broad Street - 17 Plaza
Newark, New Jersey 07101
(201) 877-7743

An important thing to remember is that a crucial purpose of associations is to help companies save on freight costs. Unfortunately, many businessmen don't even know they exist.
—Claude Wooten
Manager

SHIPPERS' ASSOCIATIONS

Shippers' Associations Pool Cargo to Reduce Freight Charges

THE PROGRAM

For years business people from all industries have formed special associations to consolidate their transportation needs and save money through volume shipping. In today's deregulated transportation environment, the expanded use of these associations is even more of a cost saver. Negotiated freight rates have become the norm, and a shippers' association can provide continuous, high-volume traffic.

Whether an association is industry specific (such as the carpet shippers' association) or handles a wide variety of goods, it works by pooling compatible cargoes with similar destinations into full truckload shipments, thus sparing many companies the higher fares they would have to pay for less-than-full loads. Further savings are also available for longer distances when associations take advantage of the "trailer-on-flatcar" or "container-on-flatcar" options provided by many railroads.

The passage of the Shipping Act of 1984 made it possible for the first time for shippers' associations to negotiate service contracts with ocean carriers. As a result the same benefits that have accrued to association members in their domestic freight arrangements are now available to them worldwide.

EVALUATION

Though savings vary depending on geographic location and shipping volume, any company that belongs to a shippers' association can expect savings of at least 10 percent in its shipping costs, and some companies have recorded savings as high as 50 percent. Shippers' associations are well protected by existing laws and are not considered in violation of any antitrust laws in their normal course of activities.

More than 150 shippers' associations are currently functioning within the United States and new associations are being organized all the time. As long as either a shipper or a receiver is a member of a shippers' association, both parties may take advantage of the cost savings that are offered.

Contact: Carole Lipsitz
Executive Assistant
American Institute for Shippers' Associations, Inc.
P.O. Box 33457
Washington, D.C. 20033
(202) 628-0933

There is a bit of irony in the fact that the software industry, which specializes in automating other technologies, has been slow in automating its own critical processes.
—Leon Presser
President

SOFTOOL CORPORATION

New Computer Program for Data Centers and Programmers Improves the Quality of the Software They Produce and Increases Productivity

THE PROGRAM

The information that is stored in computers is constantly going through change cycles that lead to new versions. Yet the inability to manage and control these changes is recognized as the single most serious obstacle to the effective utilization of computers today. It is a problem that is faced continually by software managers, developers, and users.

The Softool Corporation has become a leader in the development of a new computer discipline called Change and Configuration Management, which provides for the orderly review, testing, approval, and integration of changes like these. "Change management" helps control changes to the individual components within each software version, while "configuration management" provides control over the complete version and the relationship of its components to one another. With configuration management all components of a given product or application can be organized, managed, and tracked as a unit.

The need for effective change and configuration management is now being felt in every type of business environment. Whether we are dealing with spreadsheets, documents, graphics, or ordinary text, we are all faced with the problem of controlling revisions and managing new versions that are being produced at such a rapid pace that manual controls cannot keep up. And the larger the project or application, the faster the problem can grow out of control.

Large banks have been particularly hard hit in trying to keep their computer systems up to date with all of the new products and services being offered to customers. For many, the mere thought of yet another overhaul to implement tax withholding on interest payments almost brought many bank computer systems to a halt. The problem is not so much in the software or computers themselves, but in the process of taping together new software routines to cover new operational needs. Without adequate documentation, for which there is never enough time, it is difficult to know the effect of a new software change on those made to accommodate product changes two years ago.

As the number of people who are involved with computers continues to increase, new procedures are required that can ensure the timely coordination and notification of these changes to all those whose work is affected. Again, manual efforts are of no avail. It is essential to have an automated solution like Softool's Change and Configuration Control ("CCC") program, which is now commercially available for many different computers.

EVALUATION

Softool's CCC is a software product that addresses the many special needs of computer managers and programmers, including audit requirements, and can benefit both scientific and commercial establishments. It has become a worldwide standard for automated change and configuration management and has been instrumental in establishing a new and much-needed product category within the software products industry.

Contact: Bruce Hanna
Sales Manager
Softool Corporation
340 South Kellogg Avenue
Goleta, California 93117
(805) 683-5777

*I had one year after retirement when I did just
what you would expect—travel, luncheons,
needlepoint. But it was not enough for me. I felt
I needed to be on a schedule for structure as
well as stimulation.*

—*Evelyn Smith*
Un-retired Employee

THE TRAVELERS INSURANCE COMPANY

Un-Retirement Plan Provides Company with the Valuable
Experience and Mature Judgment of Trained and Enthusiastic
Workers

THE PROGRAM

In 1980 The Travelers Insurance Company conducted a Pre-Retirement Survey of
its 2,000 employees over age 55. Fully 85 percent of those who responded said
they were interested in some form of employment following retirement and 53
percent said that their first choice would be to work part-time for The Travelers.
Only 12 percent of the respondents reported they had done "quite a bit" to
prepare for their retirement, while 31 percent said that they had done no planning
at all.

In light of these findings, The Travelers developed its "Older Americans
Program." Its two objectives: to develop employment options for older workers
and retirees, and to help employees plan for their golden years.

The first step was to eliminate the mandatory retirement age that had been in
effect throughout the company. The second step was to identify temporary employment opportunities within the company that could be filled by qualified
retirees. Finally, positions that would lend themselves to job-sharing were targeted for those retirees who wanted to work only a few days each week. The
Board of Directors supported these initiatives by increasing from 480 to 960 the
number of hours an employee could work in a year without losing pension
benefits. A Retiree Job Bank, co-administered by two job-sharing former retirees, was also set up at company headquarters in Hartford to match retirees with
available positions.

In recent years, the Older Americans Program has been expanded to include both Travelers and non-Travelers retirees, and a recent job fair, called an "unre-tirement party," collected job applications from 300 more senior citizens. Re-tirees are also being retrained (with pay) on computerized equipment in order to keep their skills consistent with business needs.

EVALUATION

Today, 700 un-retired workers are listed in The Travelers Job Bank, helping to meet 60 percent of the company's temporary employment needs. The Travelers estimates that it saves at least $1 million a year by hiring its own retirees and relying less on more costly temporary employment agencies.

Those Travelers retirees who have returned to work say they are aware of the fact that the skills and experience they contribute make them a real asset to the company. Many of them also realize that expanded employment opportunities for older Americans increase our potential to improve both our productivity as a nation and our international competitiveness.

Contact: Barbara R. Greenberg
Manager, Older Americans Program
The Travelers Insurance Company
One Tower Square, 5 SHS
Hartford, Connecticut 06183
(203) 277-9161 or 227-2303

We seek to maximize our productivity at all levels through the proper use of capital, material, technology, and people. As part of our own principal strategies, we strive to promote effective two-way communication between employees at all levels and use new technology and management innovations to improve our operations.

—*Ray Ybaben*
Technology Manager

TRW, INC.

Electronic Mail System Speeds Decision-Making Process for Diversified Electronics Manufacturer

THE PROGRAM

At TRW, the traditional interoffice mail and telephone networks did not seem to be meeting the company's massive communication needs. So a number of corporate working committees were appointed to evaluate all the sophisticated computerized communications systems now available on the market and to establish policies and guidelines for their possible use throughout the company.

When the idea of installing an electronic mail system was suggested, a task force was formed to identify and recommend appropriate vendors and to manage the pilot project. Though TRW manufactures computer-based systems itself, it had no prior experience in this area and decided that buying a system from an outside vendor would cost less than building one from scratch, even though the company had the technical resources to do so.

The system that the company finally decided on is fully programmable and easy to use. It allows all TRW employees to mail and accept messages from company offices nationwide. Each user has a private electronic mailbox where messages are received and stored, and has only to call up the system to have the mail personally delivered.

Receiving and sending messages, however, is only one advantage of TRW's electronic mail system. It also allows documents to be edited and transmitted without having to be completely retyped and monitors pending responses without senders and receivers having to contact one another to confirm receipt of a message. Some of the system's other features:

1. Messages can be forwarded by the receiver, along with any comments to a

third party in order to answer an inquiry by the original sender.

2. Messages can be answered quickly and efficiently without both parties having to come together and without having to type formal replies.

3. Distribution lists can be standardized for any correspondence that needs to be sent to remote sales offices.

4. Any unit or department within the corporation can install its own computer bulletin board. A user has only to call up the board to find out if any new messages have been posted.

EVALUATION

At TRW employees no longer have to synchronize telephone calls, worry about the differences between time zones, or engage in the frustrating game of telephone tag. Messages can now be checked during the regular workday, during off-hours, or while on travel, and that has helped cut the time lags between conversations and final decisions by 50 percent. The new electronic mail system has decreased company communications costs by 15 to 50 percent, depending on the distances involved, and increased overall communications productivity by an estimated 25 percent. Though its benefits have not been felt to the same degree among all TRW's operating units, it has succeeded in linking them far more effectively than traditional phone calls and memos ever could.

Contact: Marsha Hopwood
Office Automation Project Manager
TRW Inc., Space Park
Redondo Beach, California
(213) 812–1828

Considerable research experience suggests that the most successful adjustments occur when workers themselves decide which training or education they prefer or is most suitable to them and when they should participate in training or in mobility programs.

—Thomas Pasco
Executive Director

UAW-FORD NATIONAL EDUCATION DEVELOPMENT AND TRAINING PROGRAM

Joint Union-Management Training Program Benefits Both Auto Manufacturer and Its Employees

THE PROGRAM

Employee training and development was recognized as a major need in the employee involvement program developed jointly by the United Auto Workers (UAW) and the Ford Motor Company. To achieve this goal, the Employee Development and Training Program was established under the 1982 collective bargaining agreement between the two parties and was expanded in the 1984 and 1987 agreements. The program is administered through the UAW-Ford National Development and Training Center in Dearborn, Michigan, and is funded at the rate of 10 cents per worker-hour by the Ford Motor Company.

This innovative joint venture recognizes the important role continued training and development plays in increasing employee skills and quality of work life. It offers over seventeen different programs to Ford's active UAW employees as well as to those who are furloughed with recall rights. The four most important programs include Education Training and Assistance, National Vocational Retraining Assistance, Targeted Vocational Retraining, and Career Counseling and Guidance. The following is a summary of the programs offered to Ford employees during 1987.

—Education fairs for 56,200 participating employees.

—Life/Education Planning Program: provided opportunities for 39,600 employees to explore their personal strengths and interests and discover new ways to increase their personal growth through education and training.

—Skills Enhancement Program: provided opportunities for 6,200 workers to continue their education, sharpen their skills in areas such as math or reading comprehension, and receive educational skills counseling.

—Education and Training Assistance Plan (ETAP): provided 25,600 employees with prepaid tuition and compulsory fees (up to a maximum of $2,000 per year) for approved self-selected education.

—Personal Development Assistance feature of ETAP: provided 13,300 employees with grants up to $1,500 per year (within ETAP allotment) for personal development and training opportunities, including noncredit or nondegree courses.

—College and University Options Program: included workshops to explore educational goals, in-plant college classes, and related support services.

—Successful Retirement Planning Program: helped 6,100 workers and their spouses to plan their transition to retirement.

—Career Day Conferences (employees involved: 7,100)

—Vocational Plans and Interest Surveys (9,100).

—Career Counseling and Guidance (9,200).

—Skills Enhancement (1,200).

—National Vocational Retraining Assistance Plan (9,800).

—Targeted Vocational Retraining Projects (1,500).

—Job Search Skills Training (4,200).

—Relocation Assistance Seminars (1,300).

—Relocation Assistance Loans (3,700).

EVALUATION

A new and unique joint effort, the UAW-Ford Employee Development and Training Program is considered to be an important contributor to Ford's recent climb to the top-earning position among U.S. automobile manufacturers. And as a result of Ford's improved performance, some 160,000 Ford workers received profit-sharing checks averaging $2,100 in 1987, based on the company's 1986 earnings.

Contact: Thomas J. Pasco
Executive Director
 or
Kenneth K. Dickinson
Executive Director
UAW-Ford National Education
  Development and Training Center
P.O. Box 6002
Dearborn, Michigan 48121
(313) 337-3464

*Having rejected the traditional approaches, we
faced a yawning void and a looming deadline.
Of necessity we came to ask the single, simple
question that provided the breakthrough: why
not measure input? In other words, why not
quantify what it takes, in human terms, to do all
the tasks our work requires—and then use that
information to determine the most appropriate
skill level for each task?*
—*Joseph Wolzansky, President*
Productivity Science Associates

WESTINGHOUSE ELECTRIC CORPORATION

Changing Business Realities Spur Nuclear Technology Division
to Staff for Service, not Design

THE PROGRAM

The people at Westinghouse's Nuclear Technology Division (NTD) knew that
their business was changing. The division was growing rapidly, but it was performing less power plant design and production work and winning more contracts
for product application and service work. Did the division really need all the
"superstar" engineers and scientists it was used to hiring? At first, no one really
knew. So management decided to begin an investigation to determine whether the
division's 3.5:1 engineer-to-technician ratio was still appropriate.

The goal was to develop a comprehensive, objective productivity plan that
could project optimal staffing requirements for the future. The program that
resulted was called Matching People and Work Requirements (MPWR) and since
work output in the NTD was nonstandardized and sporadic, input measurements
were used instead.

Staff members in the functional areas of design, analysis, testing, product
assurance, nuclear safety, and computer methods development were consulted to
determine all the discrete tasks that together defined the division's work. Employees were first surveyed to determine the time and importance of tasks they
performed in the three areas of production, service, and R&D. Then five skill
levels were matched according to the relative amount of time each would need to
perform a given task. Twenty-three computer programs were developed to analyze the information, with accounting records providing control data.

EVALUATION

The MPWR analysis revealed that the top-heavy workforce was over-qualified for much of the work that the division was now carrying out. In fact, employees had reported that 20–30 percent of their time was spent on activities that could be performed by less-skilled personnel, even though these same employees felt that the work they were doing was important and necessary. Further analysis revealed that an enormous amount of time was being spent in training people on the job primarily due to seasonal mass hirings.

The NTD decided to change its personnel practices to spread hirings throughout the year and to bring more technician-level people into the division. Within a year, the engineer-to-technician ratio had fallen to 2.7:1, and an increase in employee satisfaction levels was also noted. "Payroll costs fell the predicted 8 percent in the first year," says Charles Hoop, division program manager. "When an organization systematically matches the skills of the white-collar employees to the work required, more people do what they're best-equipped to do. And that's bound to increase productivity in human as well as financial terms."

As of the end of 1987, savings realized from the program were averaging more than $1 million per year, and the MPWR was expanded to several other divisions and support areas within Westinghouse. It has received significant publicity within the company and also served as the subject of a feature article in the *Harvard Business Review*. Since the program is applicable to environments other than engineering, aspects of it have already been applied within the health sector.

Contact: Charles C. Hoop
Configuration & Data Management
Westinghouse Electric Corporation
Marine Division
401 E. Hendy Avenue
P.O. Box 3499 (EW–1)
Sunnyvale, California 94088–3499
(408) 735–2352
    or
Joseph N. Wolzansky
President
Productivity Science Associates
6565 Penn Avenue at 5th
Pittsburgh, Pennsylvania 15206–4490
(412) 362–2000

APPENDIX

WHITE HOUSE CONFERENCE ON PRODUCTIVITY

Report

To
The President of the United States

on

PRODUCTIVITY GROWTH
A BETTER LIFE FOR AMERICA

April 1984

EXECUTIVE SUMMARY

*The challenge of greater productivity growth is of supreme
importance to America's future.* *

We are the most productive nation in the world, but our growth in productivity
has faltered. Some of the factors contributing to slower productivity growth are
within our control and some are not, but it is important that we respond to this
challenge.

Improving productivity is a necessary ingredient for providing a better life for
all Americans. Rising productivity reduces inflation and provides the opportunity
to increase real income. If America had sustained the 3.4 percent annual productivity growth rate it experienced between 1948 and 1965, the average household
would be receiving annually more than $5,000 in additional real income today. In
addition, declining productivity growth has reduced the competitiveness of
American businesses in international markets and in meeting foreign competition
in our own domestic markets. Improving productivity benefits every segment of
America: workers, managers, investors, consumers, retirees, union members,
parents, and children; but there is no separate constituency for improving productivity.

Leaders from business, labor, academia, and government assembled for the
White House Conference concluded that we can attain a higher rate of productivity growth if management and labor, and business and government, will work
together to do it.

The time for action is now; private and public sector efforts will make the
difference. Non-government sectors should focus their attention on productivity
and the factors that enhance its growth. They need to be creative, innovative, and
dedicated to achieving higher productivity. Government leaders need to assure
that economic and regulatory policies, and government production of goods and
services, support rather than impede productivity growth. If we are committed to
taking this course of action, higher productivity growth will occur.

The major findings and recommendations of the White House Conference are
highlighted in this summary. The full range of Conference deliberations can best
be appreciated by reading the section on Findings and Recommendations, the
appendices on recommendations for private sector and government action, and
the reports of the preparatory conferences.

MAJOR FINDINGS

1. *The decline in U.S. productivity growth rates that began in 1965 has
weakened America's economic vitality.*

---

*Statement by President Ronald Reagan, September 22, 1983, before the White House
Conference on Productivity.

- Low productivity growth threatens our standard of living, our competitiveness in domestic and international service and product markets, and our jobs, pay, social welfare, and defense preparedness.
- All individuals and institutions are affected and bear some responsibility for neglecting the characteristics of a productive society that made America great and for failing to evaluate the impact of their actions on productivity.

2. *The private sector—the wellspring of productivity—has suffered from many poor management and work practices and from government interference.*
   - Declining growth stems from neglect of quality, technology, productive efficiency, innovation, investment, training, planning for the future, and cooperation in the work place.
   - Our transition to a predominantly service and information based economy requires new management practices that recognize the special needs of providing value-added services.
   - Slow growth also is the result of the unnecessary burdens placed on the private sector by government.

3. *The public sector has impaired productivity growth throughout the economy.*
   - The volatile economic swings, high inflation, and rapid growth in government spending and deficits of the last two decades have created a poor environment for planning and investment in capital, human resources, and technology.
   - Large deficits in future years will raise government's consumption of loanable funds, create concerns about how government will finance its fiscal needs, and further increase the already high cost of capital.
   - The federal tax system, including social security, has become complex, cumbersome, inefficient, and a major source of disincentives for productive behavior.
   - Government's continuing intervention in private markets has failed to recognize the dynamics of our developing world economy.
   - Competition—domestic and international—is a stimulus for productivity growth, and protectionist measures tend to impede it.

4. *Total private and public investment in productivity improvement has been deficient.*
   - The high cost of capital services has held capital formation below levels required to maintain historic rates of growth in capital-labor ratios and to bring advancing technology into production through investment in new plants and equipment.
   - Training and education have not maintained the quality of the labor force and relevance necessary to meet the requirements of a rapidly changing economy.
   - The U.S. lead in discovering new knowledge and technology has not been fully transformed into developing products, nor has it been applied evenly across major sectors and industries.

5. *There is a growing recognition of the critical role that productivity plays in meeting America's economic objectives and there is early evidence that a positive change in the trend is occurring.*
   - Innovative work practices, while still too infrequent, are expanding.
   - Venture capital formation is reaching record levels.
   - While challenged, U.S. high technology industries remain competitive and are leading the world in innovation and product development, a lead which improves productivity in other industries.
   - Many companies are placing new emphasis on quality and customer demands.
   - Improving educational standards has become a national priority.
   - Rapid growth of industry-university cooperation promises future improvement in industrial technological performance.
   - Some governmental institutions have begun to recognize and relieve the burden they place on productivity growth.
   - Reduced inflation has greatly improved the environment for investment, saving, and planning.
   - There is a growing consensus that fundamental income tax reform can greatly improve productivity.

MAJOR RECOMMENDATIONS

Private Sector Action

1. *Private sector organizations should focus more attention on improving technology, quality, and information resources.* They should:
   - provide employees at all levels with necessary access to technology useful in developing new products and production processes, and keep their skills current with new technological developments through training and interaction with technology suppliers and corporate, university, and government research programs;
   - target quality as a strategic objective and reward quality improvement; and
   - treat information as a strategic asset; tie information improvement to strategic planning; and raise responsibility for information resources to the top levels of the corporate structure.
2. *Private sector managers must develop and employ creative, innovative work practices to use fully the knowledge and talent embodied in their organization's greatest resource—their employees.* They should:
   - keep employees informed about the organization's plans and respond to employee suggestions for improving market, product, and process operations;
   - tie improvement and employee rewards to company, management and employee performance through such programs as profit sharing, employee stock ownership, peer recognition, and participative management; and

- develop new skills to manage and guide the growing number of information and service workers.

3. *Private sector organizations should establish productivity measures and improvement goals for all employees, especially for information and service workers who constitute the growing majority of the workforce, and for all other measurable capital and materials resources.* They should:
   - report actual productivity results in regularly published financial and operational reports and use the estimates in the goal setting and budgeting processes of the organization; and
   - recognize the relationship between productivity measures and other organizational standards of performance such as sales, cost of product, and overhead.

4. *Labor and management must cooperate to create a workplace environment that improves productivity.* They should:
   - promote joint labor-management initiatives through committees and councils to consider workplace problems such as plant closings, restrictive work practices, training for new skills, and employment security;
   - recognize the role that labor unions must play, in organized plants, in working cooperatively with management to improve productivity and the competitiveness of the enterprise; and
   - consider joint action with government in responding to national problems such as the need to restructure the health care industry for improved efficiency and conservation of resources.

Government Action

1. *The President and the Members of Congress should seek to develop greater public recognition and acceptance of improving productivity growth as a national goal, and as the means of raising our standard of living.* They should:
   - consistently evaluate government actions, regulations, and legislation in terms of their effects on productivity in the public and private sectors;
   - create a National Medal For Productivity and Quality Achievement to recognize specific actions by organizations to improve productivity and to disseminate knowledge to others; and
   - emphasize that better techniques of measuring productivity are a vital element in the process of raising standards of living.

2. *The President and the Congress must resolve to maintain a stable, noninflationary economic environment and to reduce government's consumption of national resources.* They should:
   - make the return to fiscally responsible budget policies their first priority by reducing the rate of growth in federal spending immediately;
   - reduce government borrowing and consolidate on-budget all federal credit, loan, and loan guarantee programs; and

- set a good example of productivity improvement in their own performance by applying successful private sector productivity improvement techniques to government operations and making productivity and quality improvement a standard for evaluating government employee performance.

3. *The President and the Congress should resist making further piecemeal changes in our tax laws and develop a specific plan for fundamental tax reform.* Fundamental reform should:
   - make improving productivity a standard against which tax reform proposals are evaluated;
   - lower marginal tax rates;
   - broaden the tax base (income or consumption);
   - tax income only once by eliminating the double taxation of corporate income;
   - reduce complexity;
   - reduce tax imposed costs of capital services; and
   - achieve neutrality in effects on saving and investment decisions.

4. *The President and the Congress should enact legislation to change or repeal current laws that impose impediments to productivity growth.* They should:
   - amend environmental laws to replace technology based control requirements with performance standards;
   - require explicit cost-benefit analyses in adopting laws and regulations that impose new health, safety, and environmental requirements;
   - provide greater regulatory discretion in using market-based incentives further to improve the public health, safety, and environment;
   - amend the patent and copyright laws to protect patents and processes against unfair use by other countries, especially in the areas of computer software and chip technology;
   - amend the antitrust laws to recognize world markets as the relevant economic arena in which most U.S. companies compete;
   - revise antitrust laws to make joint ventures, including joint research and development ventures, a more effective means of meeting world competition and reducing the influence of foreign cartels on U.S. industry; and
   - continue to remove restraints on competition in the energy, communications, transportation, and financial service industries.

CALL FOR ACTION

Productivity is vital to everyone, as a public or private sector employee, taxpayer, voter, or concerned citizen. Every person needs to respond to the productivity challenge. Government can provide leadership and a catalytic stimulus, but improving the productivity of operating units in private sector and government organizations will depend on managers commitment to doing so.

Managers have a special responsibility to improve productivity. Opportunities abound in every organization, but someone must take the initiative. Talking to employees and other managers to see what has worked well in other organizations will lead to new and useful ideas. Improving productivity is not a simple task, but it need not be encumbered with the trappings of formal programs. It can begin simply with defining and rewarding good performance and emphasizing quality.

The success of the productivity effort will depend on a community effort and on cooperation among all parties. The public and private sectors will have both common and independent agendas.

The effort to improve productivity did not begin with the White House Conference on Productivity, nor should it end there. None of the recommendations and suggestions developed during the White House Conference will affect productivity growth, however, until individuals and organizations put them to use.